P9-DIH-066

THE MINISTRY OF RECONCILIATION

SPIRITUALITY & STRATEGIES

ROBERT J. SCHREITER, C.PP.S.

ORBIS BOOKS

Maryknoll, New York 10545

Tenth Printing, November 2008

Founded in 1970, Orbis Books endeavors to publish works that enlighten the mind, nourish the spirit, and challenge the conscience. The publishing arm of the Maryknoll Fathers and Brothers, Orbis seeks to explore the global dimensions of the Christian faith and mission, to invite dialogue with diverse cultures and religious traditions, and to serve the cause of reconciliation and peace. The books published reflect the views of their authors and do not represent the official position of the Maryknoll Society. To learn more about Maryknoll and Orbis Books, please visit our website at www.maryknollsociety.org.

Copyright © 1998 by Robert J. Schreiter, C.PP.S.
Published by Orbis Books, Maryknoll, New York, U.S.A.

Scripture quotations are from the New Revised Standard Version of the Bible, copyright © 1989 by the Division of Christian Education of the National Council of Churches of Christ in the United States of America and are used with permission.

Manufactured in the United States of America.

Library of Congress Cataloging in Publication Data

Schreiter, Robert J.
    The ministry of reconciliation : spirituality & strategies /
Robert J. Schreiter
        p.   cm.
    Includes bibliographical references and index.
    ISBN 1-57075-168-4 (pbk.)
    1. Reconciliation—Religious aspects—Christianity.
    2. Reconciliation—Biblical teaching.   3. Jesus Christ—Appearances.
    4. Bible. N.T. Gospels—Criticism, interpretation, etc.   5. Bible.
    N.T. Acts—Criticism, interpretation, etc.   I. Title.
    BT738.27.S34   1998
    234'.5—dc21   98-14532
                                                                    CIP

CONTENTS

PART II
ELEMENTS OF A STRATEGY FOR RECONCILIATION

INTRODUCTION

This little book continues the reflections begun in *Reconciliation: Mission and Ministry in a Changing Social Order*, published by Orbis Books in 1992. That book was written at a time when the need for social reconciliation was becoming more evident, and nations were turning to the challenge of reconstruction after a time of acute violence. At the time there was little literature available to guide those efforts. There was a good deal written about the need for reconciliation, but very little about the dynamics that would make it possible. The book *Reconciliation* was intended to add to the literature that would help promote reconciliation.

In the meantime, more literature has appeared that gives some guidance for processes of reconciliation. The most valuable are the accounts that are being written about the experience of working for reconciliation. It is still too early to try to give a systematic account of what is being learned. First of all, it is clear that we are still very much in the process of learning. There are nations such as South Africa and El Salvador where truth and reconciliation commissions are still meeting. Second, it becomes clearer as time goes on that no two situations needing reconciliation are the same. One can at best outline elements that need to be considered in undertaking reconciliation processes.

Two events in 1996 spurred me to consider writing another book on reconciliation. The first was an invitation from Antonio Baus, C.PP.S., to come to Chile in January 1997 to give a series of lectures on the occasion of the fiftieth anniversary of the presence of the Missionaries of the Precious Blood in that country. It was the Chilean experience that had first aroused my interest in the question of reconciliation. He requested that the lectures be on the resurrection because, after all the struggles to reconstruct democracy in Chile and having endured so much suffering, people needed a new source of hope. It dawned on me that the resurrection stories of the appearances of Jesus might just hold the key to hope. The lectures were presented as examples of "master narratives" into which we can put our own stories.

The second event was an invitation from Caritas Internationalis to join a working group to prepare a field manual for relief workers on reconciliation. The General Assembly of Caritas Internationalis had mandated the preparation of such a document for the use of the members of the confederation. It has been a privilege to work with such an insightful and talented group of people. For me it was an opportunity to learn a great deal from people who work directly in reconciliation processes and to think through some issues about how reconciliation happens.

The subtitle of this book is *Spirituality and Strategies*. In *Reconciliation*, I had proposed that reconciliation is more a spirituality than a strategy. It seemed to me that reconciliation had to be a way of living, had to relate to the profound spiritual issues that reconciliation raises and requires. To think of it only as strategy is to succumb to a kind of technical rationality that will succeed at best partially. Yet strategies cannot be dispensed with. Concrete experiences of struggling to achieve some measure of reconciliation require decisions, and those decisions must have some grounding. I still believe that reconciliation requires a certain spiritual orientation if it is to be successful.

The challenge of reconciliation today is such that it requires an interreligious effort. Religious difference is sometimes the cause of social conflict; in all instances, religious people must find ways to work together to achieve reconciliation. What this book hopes to offer is the spirituality that will sustain Christians in their efforts to collaborate with others in that process.

The book is in two parts. In the longer Part I, reconciliation is presented as a spirituality. The mode of presentation is a series of meditations on the Easter appearance stories of Jesus. These stories have been interpreted in many different ways. The interpretation here is that the appearances of Jesus are moments of reconciliation for the disciples. This is surely not the only way to read these stories, but I believe it is a fruitful one. Interspersed within those meditations are reflections on issues important for both a spirituality of reconciliation and strategies of reconciliation: memory, healing, forgiveness, truth, and ministry.

A much shorter Part II looks at elements of strategy in reconciliation processes. There is no attempt to look at all the possibilities for reconciliation, nor to provide a complete guide to strategies that should be considered. The reflections are limited to certain points that are essential to a Christian perspective on the reconciliation process. This is not a handbook for reconciliation, but an attempt to draw together insights that will be helpful from a Christian point of view.

There are many people who have helped me a great deal in thinking about reconciliation. Without the invitations from Antonio Baus of Chile and Jean-Luc Trouillard of Caritas Internationalis in the Vatican, this book would not have been written. Thanks to them both. Conversations with colleagues at Catholic Theological Union helped mature my thinking on different elements of what is presented here. Claude-Marie Barbour and I have had many discussions that have been extraordinarily helpful. She used an earlier draft of Part I in her seminar on ministry to survivors of human rights abuses, and the feedback from the seminar proved useful. Other colleagues whose reflections have helped me include Herbert Anderson, Dianne Bergant, Stephen Bevans, Eleanor Doidge, and Edward Foley. Doctor of Ministry students Gerard Goldman, Mark Hay, and Alicia Marill brought perspectives on reconciliation from Australia, South Africa, and the Caribbean, respectively. I am especially grateful to Mark Hay for providing materials on South Africa and for the many conversations I have had with him. Conversations at the Chicago Center for Global Ministries (Stephen Bevans, director; Richard Bliese, associate director) helped me understand situations in Rwanda and South Africa better. The working group at Caritas Internationalis, led by Duncan MacLaren, has taught me much. Group members have included Duncan MacLaren, Bishop Francisco Claver, Joseph Bock, Christine Burke, Hyo-Chong Park, Joe William, Brian

Starken, Edi Vilma Orellana, Aronet Díaz de Zamora, Timothy Radcliffe, Jean-Jacques Pérennes, Diego Cipriani, and Matteo Zuppi. Duncan MacLaren has also provided me with materials on reconciliation I would not otherwise have seen. Conversations with confreres Barry Fischer and Willi Klein have proven invaluable. Finally, thanks to Bill Burrows, my editor at Orbis Books, who has as always been constructive in his work with me, and is a dear friend. Many, many thanks to them all.

PART I

RECONCILIATION
AS
SPIRITUALITY

CHAPTER 1

Reconciliation as Spirituality

Reconciliation at the End of the Twentieth Century

The world at the end of the twentieth century is in an extraordinary state. Some would deem this to have been the most violent of all centuries known to humankind. Donald W. Schriver, Jr., reports that more than 100 million people have perished so far in wars and civil conflict.[1] Alongside those wars and conflicts must be placed authoritarian governments which have brutalized their citizens in numerous ways by imprisonment, torture, species of genocide, oppression of various kinds, and intimidation. The amount of suffering humans have inflicted upon one another in this century is both astounding and heart-rending.

The decade of the 1990s places a gruesome coda to this violent century. With the lifting of the bipolar security arrangements of the Cold War which had divided the world into two blocs, long-simmering resentments broke out in intense local conflicts. "In this decade," says Susanne Hoeber Rudolph, "the balance of violence has shifted from war 'outside,' in the anarchic space between nation states, to war 'inside,' between the embodiments of difference in civil society."[2] Conflicts within imploding nation states such as the Soviet Union and Yugoslavia

---

[1]Donald W. Schriver, Jr., *An Ethic for Enemies: Forgiveness in Politics* (New York: Oxford University Press, 1995), 9.

[2]"Introduction: Religions, States, and Transnational Civil Society," in Susanne Hoeber Rudolph and James Piscatori (eds.), *Transnational Religion and Fading States* (Boulder, CO: Westview Press, 1997), 4.

and the ethnic slaughters in Rwanda point to another level of violence. It has become a kind of truism in relief agency work that, up until the late 1980s, most of the disasters that needed relief were natural catastrophes caused by earthquakes, hurricanes, and storms. Now the number of disasters to which relief workers struggle to respond has increased fivefold—and they are nearly all of human fabrication. Previously relief work meant the alleviation of physical human misery. Now it must attend also to the healing of human societies riven by violence and hatred. Some form of social reconciliation must be sought.

The reconciliation called for presents two faces. One face is social. It has to do with providing structures and processes whereby a fractured society can be reconstructed as truthful and just. It has to do with coming to terms with the past, punishing wrongdoers, and providing some measure of reparation to victims. It must create a secure space and an atmosphere of trust that makes civil society possible.

The other face is spiritual. It has to do with rebuilding shattered lives so that social reconciliation becomes a reality. The state can set up commissions to examine the wrongdoing of the past, but it cannot legislate the healing of memories. The state can offer amnesty or mete out punishment to wrongdoers, but it cannot guarantee forgiveness. Social reconciliation sets up conditions that make reconciliation more likely, but those conditions cannot of themselves effect it. That is why secular NGOs (non-governmental organizations) frequently turn to their religious counterparts and ask for help with this necessary spiritual dimension. Most religious NGOs find themselves caught off guard, and they too must seek help for this spiritual dimension. Reconciliation had not been part of their portfolio either. Many cultures have ways of reincorporating wrongdoers and deviants into their communities. Some Christian churches have rites and sacraments of reconciliation. But reconciliation in the many different places and on the scale the world now needs remains an elusive spiritual practice.

The first part of this book looks at the spiritual dimensions of reconciliation from a Christian perspective. It is intended to explore those dimensions both at the level of those who have lived through violence and are now seeking healing for themselves, and at the level of those who accompany them in a ministry of reconciliation.

This will be done principally via a long-standing spiritual practice, a Christian way of dealing with suffering. It involves bringing one's own story of suffering into contact with the story of the suffering, death, and resurrection of Jesus Christ. Sometimes that encounter involves placing one's story inside the Jesus story, a practice Christians call uniting their suffering to the suffering of Christ. If Christ's suffering was redeeming for a sinful and conflicted world, then perhaps my suffering can gain meaning by being united to Christ's suffering.

At other times, looking at how Jesus dealt with his own suffering provides a way of understanding the suffering that people are now undergoing. Then suffering takes on the marks of a discipleship, or a walking with Jesus in suffering. If the first practice creates a kind of inner, spiritual union in suffering, this second practice creates an identification in action.

To arrive at a better understanding of the spiritual dimension of reconciliation, this first part of the book will focus on one part of the story of Jesus' suffering, death, and resurrection. It will explore the stories of the appearances of Jesus after the resurrection as recounted in the gospels. By examining Jesus' actions in these stories, we hope to gain insight into the spirituality of reconciliation: how reconciliation is experienced, how that experience can become a key to a new way of living, and how that way of living might be shared with and transmitted to others. A focus on the stories of Jesus' suffering and death might provide a helpful way of enduring suffering. But it does not explore adequately how we might be released from the bonds of suffering. The passion and death tell us of the depths to which suffering can draw people down, but it does not give any picture of what a new life, redeemed and liberated from that suffering, might look like. The gospel stories of Jesus' passion and death—stories of betrayal, humiliation, torture, and abandonment, culminating in his execution as an enemy of the state—may tell us how to act in face of violence. If God did indeed raise Jesus up to a new life which breaks the grip of violence and sin on the world, what then should be the concrete object of our hope? The proposal that is being made here is that the appearance stories can be read as practices of reconciliation, of coming to terms with a violent history, and of building the beginnings of a new humanity and a new community.

Just how the appearance stories might provide us greater spiritual insight into reconciliation will be addressed shortly. To prepare for that, however, two preliminary steps must be taken.

The first involves being more aware of the kinds of conditions under which reconciliation takes place in many societies today as they try to rebuild. This might seem a digression into the social dimension of reconciliation, but it is a necessary one. Reconciliation never happens in a vacuum. Not attending to what type of reconciliation is sought in a situation and to the expectations for achieving it can hamper or even thwart the process. It is necessary, then, to see how the meaning of reconciliation itself changes as a society moves through the transition from outright violence and conflict into efforts to heal and rebuild. Misidentifying what reconciliation "should" be can delay any progress toward its actual completion.

The second preliminary step is to talk about the principal features of a Christian understanding of reconciliation. Reconciliation means many different things. In divorce courts, reconciliation means the end of the separation of an estranged couple. Sometimes the term is a codeword for a certain kind of justice. For conflict mediators it can mean the cessation of hostility. What does reconciliation mean within the Christian tradition? Even within Christianity there is no uniform definition or focus. Since the purpose of this book is not to address the full range of what reconciliation is and might be, but rather to focus on the Christian contribution, it is important that we establish as clearly as possible just what that Christian understanding is.

With that done, the stage will be set to look at how the resurrection stories might yield for us a deeper understanding of a spirituality of reconciliation.

Phases in the Reconciliation Process

Amnesty International worker Daan Bronkhorst traveled the world in the mid-1990s to gather information on what people were learning about the reconciliation process. On the basis of his research he proposed that societies tend to go through three phases in their transition from trauma to reconciliation.[3] Knowledge of what phase a society is in will help in understanding what people think reconciliation is and in assessing the general expectations about what measures of reconciliation might be achieved. What he has presented is expanded here to help focus upon what Christian reconciliation might mean in this process.

The first phase Bronkhorst calls the *genesis phase*. In this phase, the shifts in relations of power in a conflicted society are getting under way. It becomes clear to all that major change is in the offing. There is growing internal instability, as those who have been oppressed become more and more assertive against their oppressors. The restive migration out of East Germany in early 1989 that showed up the slackening grip of the German Democratic Republic over its people was an example of this. The growing militancy against apartheid in South Africa in the late 1980s was another example. Sometimes the instability is heightened by the cooperation of a foreign government with the rising militancy, either actively (such as Austria and then West Germany opening its borders to East Germans), or passively (Gorbachev's decision not to intervene on East Germany's behalf). There is a sense then that confrontation is coming and some change will have to take place.

Any calls for reconciliation at this turbulent, genesis phase are early, distant alerts about challenges still lying in the future. What will happen is still so unclear that it is hard to imagine how it all might be resolved. Such calls for reconciliation as there are frequently come from church authorities who foresee what is coming. The calls are cast in very general terms, and usually do not gain much hearing. Thus, the Roman Catholic bishops of Chile were speaking about reconciliation already in 1985, even though the transition to democracy did not come until several years later. Sometimes church leaders will speak of reconciliation at this early stage in the hope of curbing the vio-

---

[3] Daan Bronkhorst, *Truth and Reconciliation: Obstacles and Opportunities for Human Rights* (Amsterdam: Amnesty International, 1995), 31-32.

lence that seems likely to ensue. At any rate, during this phase, reconciliation is seen as something that will be necessary, but its exact character—and how to achieve it—remains quite abstract.

The second phase is the *transformation phase*. This is the actual beginning of the transition. It is usually marked by some event that takes on major symbolic significance as a turning point. The fall of the Berlin Wall in 1989 was such an event in Europe. The release of Nelson Mandela from prison in South Africa was another. The event carries with it the meaning that there can now be no turning back to the old way of doing things.

What often follows this symbolic moment are events that happen in such rapid succession that people have to struggle to keep up with them. A new government replaces the old. Forces that had been oppressed or in opposition suddenly find themselves in power. The volatile and even chaotic character of the events marks a great release of social energy that is often accompanied by great creativity as expectations of genuine social change grow. The creativity shows itself in the grand sweep of visions for a reconciled future and a radically reconstructed society, visions that are presented by leaders, by poets, and frequently by youth. In this phase, it seems possible to imagine and even to achieve a thoroughly reconstructed society, and that possibility galvanizes the energies of large sectors of the population. Those visions usually—and accurately—diagnose what ills need to be addressed, but do not offer many specifics about how to address them. There is simply no time to ponder such details.

Reconciliation is experienced at this stage as the *possibility* of reconciliation. This possibility feels more immediate than the pronouncements made in the genesis phase. Things continue to move so fast, however, that there is little time to plot any plan or program of reconciliation.

The third phase is the *readjustment phase*. After the excitement of the transformation phase, the reconstruction of society begins. It is usually marked by a twofold strategy. On the one hand, there is a struggle to hold onto and consolidate the changes that have taken place. This was evident in Eastern Europe where, although countries embraced democracy, the people in those countries had little or no experience of how to live in a democratic society. Often, too, although a major transition may have taken place, the powerful figures of the old regime are still around. Even after he relinquished the presidency in a democratic election, General Pinochet continued as commander of the armed forces in Chile, thereby subjecting democratically elected leaders to a relentless scrutiny. The Communists may have relinquished leadership in one Eastern European country after another, but there are still Communists at every level of government and society, and their sympathies are known. The new government, then, cannot simply stride ahead with its reforms. It must be constantly checking its back for reactions from the defeated, but not disengaged, powers of the old regime.

But nonetheless (and this is the second part of the strategy) steps have to be taken to implement elements of the vision of the future (sometimes there are competing visions) that had emerged in the transition phase as the new ideal society. It seems as though everything has to be done at once, often with very few human and economic resources. Wrongdoers have to be brought to justice, reparation has to be made to victims, and new structures and processes for society have to be put in place—seemingly all at the same time. Not only is there a shortfall of trained people for one or more aspects of the task (there were almost no judges available to preside at the trials in Rwanda after the hostilities had ended), but the more sinister dimensions of society start to emerge from the shadows and consume great amounts of energy. In the former East Germany people were transfixed by the opening of the Stasi files which brought to light the extent of surveillance of the State and the collaboration of so many citizens. In South Africa, the sessions of the Truth and Reconciliation Commission in 1996 and 1997 consumed the nation's attention with their revelations of human rights violations. Realization of the extent and depth of violence and evil perpetrated on a citizenry makes apparent how much will have to be made right before a just society can be built. What becomes clearer in this is how difficult a complete turn-around of a society will be. The phoenix arises from the ashes only in the myth.

Part of the problem is that the transformation and the re-building of a society are never self-contained. Outside forces begin to impinge on the designs of leadership for change. East Germany, for example, hoped that after unification it could maintain some of its autonomy in the new Germany and create a society that would be a kind of "third way" between capitalism and socialism. But the reunification occurred entirely on West German terms. The influx of neoliberal capitalism with its global markets may thrust aside plans for a new, more equitable economic organization, dragging a vulnerable economy into the maelstrom of economic globalization. Likewise, other elements inside the society may take advantage of the chaos for their own ends. Crime rose dramatically in Russia and in South Africa after the transitions in those countries. The rise in crime was both emblematic of the chaos and breakdown of order and an expression of anarchic striving to enrich oneself quickly at others' expense. Evil had metamorphosed into a new form.

Constant chaos can be exhausting. The ideals that once galvanized people of diverse interests, uniting them in acts of resistance and in the struggle for liberation, no longer hold things together. One part of the problem is that it is easier to galvanize collective negative emotion *against* something or someone than it is to organize collective positive emotion *for* something or someone.[4] The coalition of resistance falls apart as disagreements grow about what the future should be and how soon it should be realized. Another part of the problem results from weariness. As disillusionment about the future sets in, people turn away from the challenges of nation-building and devote themselves to private pursuits. This may mean laying aside the self-sacrifice that resistance required to concentrate on getting rich, or loosening the restraints imposed by an authoritarian government to plunge headlong into consumerism and the fulfillment of desire. This is often seen in the young, who brought such single-minded energy to the transformation but now feel betrayed by the ambivalences of the readjustment phase.

---

[4] I owe this expression to Joseph G. Bock, who was reflecting on the fomenting and prevention of communal violence in the Indian subcontinent.

There grows a collective sense of wanting to forget the past or at least gain distance from it. A call to get on with life instead of dwelling on a past that might again fracture the fragile unity that has been achieved gains more and more hearing.

For others, the continuing chaos is too much to bear, and they seek out ethnic, nationalist, or religious movements that promise security in the face of what seems a world out of control. The rise of all three of these types of movements after the dissolution of the Soviet Union was much in evidence. Here clarity wins out over truth: a single group (immigrants, foreigners) is held responsible for an unstable situation that in reality has many causes.

Even when stability is achieved and economic prosperity becomes more likely, there may be a general mood of disappointment about how things have turned out, how partial or fragmentary the change has really been. A relatively short transformation phase, marked by excitement about the future, turns into a long readjustment phase that will take years, even decades. That realization may create depression and resignation in large sectors of society.

It is during the readjustment phase that programs of reconciliation are carried out. They often begin with the excitement and energy of the transformation phase, but gradually come to bear the burdens of the readjustment phase just outlined here. In trying to find out just what happened in the years of oppression and wrongdoing, the picture gets more and more complex. The human rights violations and other crimes become more difficult to untangle. The evils of that time spill back into earlier times, blurring the line about when all the trouble really began. The German theologian Dietrich Bonhoeffer, imprisoned and executed by the Nazis, captures well the frustrations and the fears of those struggling to rebuild a society:

> We have been silent witnesses of evil deeds. Many storms have gone over our heads. We have learnt the art of deception and of equivocal speech. Experience has made us suspicious of others, and prevented us from being open and frank. Bitter conflicts have made us weary and even cynical. Are we still of any use? ... Will our spiritual

reserves prove adequate and our candour with ourselves remorseless enough to enable us to find our way back again to simplicity and straightforwardness?[5]

People will lose interest in reconciliation programs and become cynical about the possibility of their ever achieving their goal. People will want to get on with their lives, but find it hard to do so. At this point, many may question whether reconciliation is even worth the effort, as the reconstructing society appears to be impotent in punishing wrongdoers and effecting real change. At the same time, however, there is a great yearning to find a way of deliverance from the memories of the past and the sufferings of the present.

In the readjustment phase, reconciliation can no longer afford to be abstract. There are concrete instances of violations of human rights to be addressed, there are survivors to be cared for, there are amnesties and pardons to complicate matters: in all of this reconciliation seems to be ever more elusive. The fragmentary realization of any reconciliation reminds Christians that reconciliation is ultimately the work of God and the gift of God. That does not mean that people striving for reconciliation should give up their efforts and sit idly by. It is but a reminder of the sheer enormity of the task and the impossibility of any human effort to encompass it completely. What becomes key for Christians involved in reconciliation—either as victims or as ministers of the reconciliation—is to understand how they interact with the work of God and how they become instruments of God's work in all of this.

It is important that those who are seeking reconciliation in their own lives, and those who work for reconciliation, are aware of these transition phases and what each means for the ministry of reconciliation. As should be evident, the challenge is especially compelling in the readjustment phase, when energies may increasingly fragment or flag. It is here that an articulated spirituality to sustain the reconciliation process becomes ever more important.

---

[5]Dietrich Bonhoeffer, *Letters and Papers from Prison* (New York: Macmillan, 1962), 34.

To lay the groundwork for such a spirituality of reconciliation, we need first to review elements of the Christian understanding of reconciliation.

The Christian Understanding of Reconciliation

There is no agreed upon definition of reconciliation in human societies. One reason for this is that the specific circumstances for which reconciliation is needed have a profound effect on the very meaning of reconciliation itself. Who needs to be involved, what needs to be overcome or undone, what will count for truth and justice in the new situation, and what is deemed to be the end of the process: all of these affect what reconciliation means. Some cultures have a very distinct concept of reconciliation that is expressed ritually: an accusation of wrongdoing is leveled at someone, that person acknowledges the wrongdoing and apologizes in some formal way, the apology is accepted by the community, and the wrongdoer is ritually reintegrated into the community, signifying forgiveness. Sometimes a probationary period marked by ritual punishment (such as a fine or a continuing partial exclusion from the community) precedes full reintegration. This pattern is reenacted in myriad variations throughout the world.

The Christian understanding of reconciliation has had many different meanings. As Cilliers Breytenbach has pointed out, context and circumstances have affected how Christians have used the word reconciliation and how they have gone about achieving it.[6]

In a thoughtful reflection on diverse Christian understandings of reconciliation, Gregory Baum has pointed to different perspectives of Protestants and Catholics in contemporary discussions.[7] Expanding on his insights here, one could say that,

---

[6]Cilliers Breytenbach, "Reconciliation: Shifts in Christian Soteriology," in W. S. Vorster (ed.), *Reconciliation and Reconstruction: Creative Options for a Rapidly Changing South Africa* (Pretoria: University of South Africa Press, 1986), 1-25.

[7]"A Theological Afterword," in Gregory Baum and Harold Wells (eds.), *The Reconciliation of Peoples: Challenge to the Churches* (Maryknoll, NY: Orbis Books, 1997), 184f.

for Protestants, there is an emphasis on reconciliation as the result of Christ's atoning death and the justification by faith. By focusing on the atoning death, this position has the advantage of seeing reconciliation in continuity with the saving acts of God through history, especially in a theology of covenant. If there is a classic location for a Protestant theology of reconciliation, it is Romans 5:6-11.

The Catholic emphasis would be slightly different, focusing on the love of God poured out upon us as a result of the reconciliation God has effected in Christ. Here the emphasis is on the new creation. If there is a classic location for this theology, it is 2 Corinthians 5:17-20.

In the description of a Christian understanding of reconciliation that follows here, the emphasis favors the Catholic position. Let me summarize what I see as the central points of Paul's teaching on reconciliation in five points:[8]

First of all, *reconciliation is the work of God, who initiates and completes in us reconciliation through Christ.* Ultimately, reconciliation is not a human achievement, but the work of God within us. From what was just said about the challenges to reconciliation in the readjustment phase of a country's transition, it should be apparent how enormous, complex, and nearly impossible the task of reconciliation is. What will reconciliation mean finally for South Africa, for Guatemala and El Salvador, for the countries of the former Soviet Bloc? All of these are situations that appear to exceed our capacity to change completely.

Furthermore, God initiates the work of reconciliation in the lives of the victims. Ordinarily we would expect reconciliation to begin with the repentance of the wrongdoers. But experience shows that wrongdoers are rarely willing to acknowledge what they have done or to come forward of their own accord. If reconciliation depended entirely upon the wrongdoers' initiative, there would be next to no reconciliation at all.

---

[8]For a more extended treatment of Paul's theology of reconciliation in the framework of these five points, see Robert J. Schreiter, *Reconciliation: Mission and Ministry in a Changing Social Order* (Maryknoll, NY: Orbis Books, 1992), 41-62; idem, art. "Reconciliation," in Karl Müller, Theo Sundermeier, Stephen B. Bevans, and Richard Bliese (eds.), *Dictionary of Mission: Theology, History, Perspectives* (Maryknoll, NY: Orbis Books, 1997), 379-82.

God begins with the victim, restoring to the victim the humanity which the wrongdoer has tried to wrest away or to destroy. This restoration of humanity might be considered the very heart of reconciliation. The experience of reconciliation is the experience of grace—the restoration of one's damaged humanity in a life-giving relationship with God. Humans are created in the image and likeness of God (Gen 1:26). It is that image by which humanity might mirror divinity, by which humanity comes into communion with divinity, that is restored. That God would begin with the victim, and not the evildoer, is consistent with divine activity in history. God takes the side of the poor, the widowed and the orphaned, the oppressed and the imprisoned. It is in the ultimate victim, God's son Jesus Christ, that God begins the process that leads to the reconciliation of the whole world in Christ (Col 1:20).

In like manner, God begins the process of human reconciliation with the victim. It is through the victim that the wrongdoer is called to repentance and forgiveness. Seen from this perspective, repentance and forgiveness are not the preconditions for reconciliation, but are rather the consequences of it. This paradoxical thought will be explored in further detail in the sections on forgiveness below.

This emphasis on God's initiative could lead some to assume that human activity contributes nothing to the reconciliation process. They would say that therefore there is no point in trying to engage in the work of reconciliation. Or the wrongdoer might say, I cannot repent until God touches my heart... or the victim might say, I cannot forgive until God moves me to do so. The problem with this line of thinking is that it creates a too simple dichotomy between divine and human action. God's action is not some thunderbolt over and apart from human action. The communion between the human and the divine involves divine initiative coming through human action. It is frequently reported that the moment of reconciliation comes upon the victim as a surprise, or the consequences of reconciliation take people where they had not expected to go. There one can discern God's action: moving the victim and the community along in a moment of grace.

Discovering that moment of intersection of the divine and the human leads to the second point in a Christian understanding of reconciliation, namely, *reconciliation is more a spirituality than a strategy*. If reconciliation is principally God's work, then we are but "ambassadors for Christ" (2 Cor 5:20). It is in God working through us that reconciliation is to be found. Reconciliation means in the first instance, then, the cultivation of a relationship with God that becomes the medium through which reconciliation can happen. That relationship expresses itself in spiritual practices that create space for truth, for justice, for healing, and for new possibilities. Such practices lead to creating communities of memory, safe places to explore and untangle a painful past, and the cultivation of truth-telling to overcome the lies of injustice and wrongdoing. They lead also to creating communities of hope, where a new future might be imagined and celebrated. Often reconciled victims—and sometimes other members of reconciling communities—receive a call or vocation to become healers of others: healers of other victims, healers of wrongdoers. That healing takes place through the practice of truth-telling, the pursuit of justice, and peace-making.

Reconciliation as a spirituality is absolutely essential. The chapters in the rest of Part I of this book explore dimensions of that spirituality: how to practice it, how to cultivate it. Reconciliation is also, however, about strategies. Creating the conditions under which reconciliation might happen in communities of memory and communities of hope is the first step of any reconciliation strategy. But there are other things that can be done to promote reconciliation. Part II of this book will look at elements of strategies. Among those strategies are the discernment of similarities and differences between individual and social reconciliation, the promoting of truth-telling and forgiveness, the use of ritual moments, and practices of peace-making.

Strategies of reconciliation cannot be bypassed in a ministry of reconciliation. First of all, the experience of reconciliation is not simply the opportunity to dwell in the overwhelming grace of God; it leads to action. That action is embodied in strategies that support and promote the reconciliation process. Second, because social reconciliation always remains incomplete, intermediate structures and processes will always be needed to rebuild and sustain the social fabric. How laws are to be formulated, how amnesty and pardon are to be judiciously used to strengthen a new society, how justice is to be understood and implemented: all of these require strategic thinking and action.

Recognition of the relation between spirituality and strategy is essential in countering problems that frequently arise in the ministry of reconciliation. A concentration on strategy without an equal emphasis on spirituality gives the impression that reconciliation is a technique that can be learned. Reconciliation becomes something that human beings can do in and of themselves. Especially for people from wealthy countries, used to working with many resources, such an understanding of reconciliation leads to a hubris that will cause efforts at reconciliation to fail. Many meetings and conferences on reconciliation founder precisely for this reason: it is as though reconciliation is one more thing we can do for ourselves if we can only get the strategy right. Anyone who has been in the presence of the great human wreckage at the end of dictatorships, or of the civil wars at the end of the twentieth century draws back instinctively from such hubris.

There is, then, a balance between spirituality and strategy. A spirituality that does not lead to strategies does not fulfill its goal. A strategy that is not based in a spirituality will fall short of the mark. There must be this mutual interaction. In that interaction it is the spirituality that should guide the strategy, even as the strategy gives the spirituality form in action and practice.

Third, *the experience of reconciliation makes of both victim and wrongdoer a new creation* (2 Cor 5:17). Reconciliation was described above as the restoration of our humanity. The experience of God's reconciling work is such that restoration does not mean taking us back to our former state, the condition in which we were before evil was done. It is restoration in the sense that God gives us back the humanity that was wrested from us, but it is a humanity that includes now the experience of reconciliation. It is not a denial or obliteration of the painful experience of injustice and violation; it is a transformation of the experience that will be forever part of who we are. Reconciliation is not about the erasure of memory; it is about its transformation. This will be explored in greater detail in the chapters on memory and forgiveness below.

It is important to stress this point, because strategies of reconciliation that operate without this spirituality see reconciliation as a restoration of the *status quo ante.* They see justice in the same light: restitution. But so often that earlier status is gone forever, and so beyond our reach. And who can do justice for the dead? Reconciliation is not about going back. It is about addressing the past adequately so that we can go forward.

That going forward is not something we can construct entirely for ourselves. If we could, reconciliation would be reduced to a strategy. The fact that the outcome of reconciliation is so often a surprise, both for victims and for entire communities, is an experience of that "new creation." Victims find themselves in a new place, often with a vocation to heal others. Communities find themselves also in a new place where they had not expected to be.

This new creation of both victim and wrongdoer is a sign of God's presence. The victim's restored humanity must include the painful experience of violence, because that is now part of the victim's memory and identity. But it is transformed toward a new end. This will be explored in more detail in the discussion of Jesus' healing wounds in chapter 5.

Fourth, *the process of reconciliation that creates the new humanity is to be found in the story of the passion, death, and resurrection of Jesus Christ.* As was said above, for Christians, the "master narrative" of divine reconciliation is found in the story of Christ's suffering, death, and resurrection. Our narratives of suffering, of experience of violence and violation, can find their form and their transformation in the story of what God has done in Christ. His passion and death are recounted, not for the gruesome and unjust treatment they were, but as a "dangerous memory"[9] of how God subverted power that was used for perpetrating injustice. The resurrection confirms and manifests God's power over evil, which is why we are able to read the resurrection stories as stories of God's healing and forgiving power in the world.

---

[9] The phrase is Johannes Baptist Metz's. See his *Befreiendes Gedächtnis Jesu Christi* (Mainz: Matthias-Grünewald-Verlag, 1970).

We look then to the Paschal Mystery—that pathway from suffering to death and then to new life—as the narrative that organizes our chaotic and painful experience of violence into a narrative that will carry us, too, from death to life. It is this yearning that is echoed in Paul's cry in the letter to the Philippians: "I want to know Christ and the power of his resurrection and the sharing of his sufferings by becoming like him in his death, if somehow I may attain the resurrection from the dead" (Phil 3:10-11).

Fifth, *the process of reconciliation will be fulfilled only with the complete consummation of the world by God in Christ.* As we become aware of the complexity that must be untangled in a reconciliation process, and the enormity of the task of doing this, we are humbled before the charge to bring about reconciliation. It becomes ever more evident that reconciliation is God's work, with our cooperation. The final state of reconciliation, that new creation, is not the inexorable unfolding of a preconceived scheme programmed to happen from the very beginning. It involves human agency, and the coming together of a myriad of contingent events. Reconciliation can only be grasped as involving "all things, whether on earth or in heaven, by making peace through the blood of his cross" (Col 1:20).

The Resurrection Stories as Stories of Reconciliation

Having examined the phases of transition in societies and how these affect reconciliation, and having explored what Christians mean by reconciliation, we can return to the resurrection stories as stories of reconciliation. Stories are powerful means for shaping our identities. They weave together in a narrative the events that have special significance for us. By moving persons as actors and actresses along the story line, they allow different aspects of their personalities and characters to emerge. The drama of the story helps us remember its content more easily than if that content were stored in concepts.

Our identities are based strongly on the stories we tell about ourselves, our families, our friends, our communities, our countries. In these collections of stories, stories about origins hold a special place. They often embody the fundamental values that we see unfolding in the rest of our history. Stories of facing and overcoming adversity likewise hold a special place for us. Those incidents in which we seem to transcend ourselves give us a special insight into who we are.

Significant too about the best of our stories is that they can be recast as our contexts change and as we gain new insights into ourselves and our communities. That does not mean that they are total fabrications or are completely subject to our whims. It means, rather, that they are not just accounts of the past, but are living parts of us now. The retelling of the stories is not so much about changing them as it is about gaining new perspective. Often that new perspective helps us understand our current situation better.

As has already been noted above, the stories of Jesus have this powerful effect for Christians and indeed for many others. For Christians the stories are a special window into God's activity in the world. They give us clues as to who God is and what God is trying to communicate to us.

The stories connected with the Paschal Mystery—the suffering, death, and resurrection of Jesus—stand central in all of this. They offer a matrix for understanding what true power is, what suffering and death mean, how evil is overcome, and what we may hope for from God. Philippians 3:10-11, quoted above, captures Paul's sentiment about this: "I want to know Christ and the power of his resurrection and the sharing of his sufferings by becoming like him in his death, if somehow I may attain the resurrection from the dead." We hear in Paul a craving for a deeper knowledge (what he calls elsewhere the "surpassing knowledge of my Lord Jesus Christ"). This was the Paul who had not known the historical Jesus of Nazareth; his experience had been that of the Risen One. That experience is hinted at in his speaking of the "power" of the resurrection, a dynamic and transforming energy that does more than reconstitute things as they were before. It brings an utter transfiguration of beings.

Paul knew too that the key to knowing Christ, to experiencing Christ's resurrection, was through his suffering and death. To be transfigured with Christ in his glory, we must be configured with him into his death. We must take on the form of

Christ, as Christ took on our own form (cf. Phil 2:6-7). One cannot experience the power of the resurrection without having known the cross.

It is because Paul links understanding of the resurrection with understanding of Jesus' suffering and death that I would propose that the stories of the post-resurrection appearances of Jesus can be read as stories of reconciliation. Throughout the history of Christianity the appearance stories have been read in many different ways. Early in the twentieth century, for example, theological students saw the appearance stories as proofs of the divinity of Jesus. In the latter part of the same century, many theological students wondered whether these stories reflected historical experiences of the disciples or whether they represented parables of belief, conversion, and mission. It is clear that the accounts found in the four gospels and in 1 Corinthians 15:3-8 cannot be harmonized into a single narrative.

The fact that these stories can be read in so many different ways points to their narrative power, their capacity for shaping our identity. It is precisely this power that draws me to them as narratives of reconciliation. They address the effects of the shameful torture and death of Jesus, the trauma created in the lives of his disciples. The appearances of Jesus are moments of recognition, of reconciliation, and of healing. They are moments of recognition of the pain, the loss, and the guilt of the disciples: the pain and confusion of the two disciples on the way to Emmaus; the loss felt so keenly by Mary Magdalene; the guilt of Peter for having denied Jesus, and the guilt of the male disciples for having deserted him. They are moments of reconciliation and forgiveness for a doubting Thomas and a remorseful Peter. They are moments of healing for everyone, helping them overcome their timidity and fear in order to regroup and carry on Jesus' mission.

I think that reading the resurrection appearance stories as stories of reconciliation can give us a host of hints about the nature of reconciliation as a spirituality, as a ministry, and as a strategy. In the six chapters that follow, appearance stories will be recounted to discover deeper meanings about reconciliation. To be sure, this is not the only way to read the appearance stories; it simply reflects their richness and multivalent character. Some might object that this is a kind of reading into the appearance stories what we want to see. That is a danger, but one I hope is not entered into here. What these reflections on the appearance stories are meant to be are examples of how we can bring our own stories of quests for reconciliation to the Jesus story. This is something that characterizes the Christian practice of reconciliation, as noted in the fourth point above. We bring our quests for reconciliation to the Paschal Mystery in the hope that our quests might be illumined, and our horizons expanded.

The Risen Lord as Victim and Reconciler

One final thing should be noted about the appearance stories of the resurrection as stories of reconciliation. If God starts with the victim, who then on God's behalf reaches out to others, who is the victim in the appearance stories? It is none other than Jesus himself. Restored to life in a transfigured humanity, he now begins by healing and forgiving his disciples, commissioning them in turn to carry forth his message and mission to the whole world.

Approaching the stories in this manner gives us an unusual perspective on the appearances of Jesus. We usually focus upon what they mean for the disciples, since we as latter-day disciples hope to discern some pattern for ourselves. The perspective taken here invites us to view the stories from the side of Jesus, the reconciled victim. What did these encounters with his disciples, what did the experience of forgiving, comforting, and healing, mean for him? Of course, we cannot get into the mind and feelings of Jesus. While it may seem presumptuous for us to even try to imagine what it meant for Jesus, I believe the stories invite us to do so, so that we can come to know better, with Paul, the power of Christ's resurrection.

CHAPTER 2

What the Women Saw

(Mark 16:1-8; John 20:1-18)

Dawn is just breaking. Three women walk hurriedly down a road, paying little attention to anything around them. It has been a difficult three days. On Friday they had been witnesses to an execution—a slow, painful, and humiliating death. They were living in an occupied country, and the state power maintained itself by these fearsome deeds of violence. They were staged in public places, along a road, or sometimes in the garbage dump, to mark those executed as human rubbish. There they would be taunted by passers-by, to be humiliated even more. The condemned were hanged on a cross until they became so weakened that they asphyxiated.

The man executed that Friday had been so good to them. He had been a teacher, and had permitted them to follow in his company, something usually allowed only to men. He had changed the life of one of them, Mary Magdalene, by healing her of a great affliction. Another of them, also called Mary, was the mother of James, a close disciple of the executed man. She wondered whether her son was safe.

The women reach the goal of their short journey, an outcropping of rock that had been hollowed out for a tomb. There on Friday night they had watched the hasty interment of the executed man. Usually the bodies of the executed were cut down from their crosses and thrown into the garbage dump, the final humiliation: they were not even accorded a simple, decent burial. But an influential admirer of the executed man had gotten permission from the authorities to bury the body, and so the executed man had been laid in this simple tomb. They were grateful that he had been granted at least this simple dignity after so much humiliation. They were coming now to render him that final homage of preparing the body for its rest.

Now something was wrong. The stone that sealed the opening in the rock had been rolled back. The body was gone! Had the rulers changed their minds, and taken the body away to be disposed of in some unknown place? Would their gentle leader become one of the "disappeared," after so humiliating and excruciating a death? What were they to do? Mark's account ends by saying that they "fled from the tomb, for terror and amazement had seized them; and they said nothing to anyone, for they were afraid" (16:8).

The Women of the Resurrection

All four gospels recount that Jesus first appeared to women after his resurrection. Only 1 Corinthians gives a different account, according to which Jesus appeared first to Cephas (15:3-8). In several of the accounts, the men did not believe the women's story. As is still the case in so many societies today, women were not seen as reliable witnesses. In those societies, women's domain is the home and not the public forum.

Jesus had treated them differently. He had allowed them to travel with him in his itinerant preaching, seeing to the feeding and care of that little band. He treated them with a dignity and respect that they had not often experienced. He even taught them, showing respect for their minds and their thinking. He had insisted that in the reign of God to come, things would be reversed. Those at the margins would take center stage. Those considered to be the least would become the greatest.

Being marginal and insignificant had had its advantages as well. The male disciples of Jesus had scattered at Jesus' arrest. That may seem cowardly, but when it became known that Jesus was to be executed by crucifixion, it was a matter of survival. Crucifixion as a form of capital punishment was reserved for enemies of the state. If Jesus was seen as an insurgent, then his immediate followers ran the risk of being crucified with him. That was what had happened to Judas the Galilean and his followers four years earlier, when he and forty-two of his followers were crucified together.

Because the state paid no attention to women, they were able to follow along at a distance as Jesus was led out of the city gates. They were able to keep vigil, to hear his cries of pain as he hung on the cross. It did not take long. Sometimes those crucified took several days to die. But Jesus had been so weakened by his torture and beatings that he was soon exhausted to the point of death.

Now the women who had been with him at his death witness something puzzling and disconcerting. *He is not here.* In the account of the gospel of Mark, they hurry away full of fear. What does that mean, "He has been raised"? In the gospel of John, it is only Mary Magdalene at the tomb. There we hear her plaintive words, "They have taken away my Lord, and I do not know where they have laid him" (20:13).

Those women who kept vigil at Jesus' death are now the witnesses to the resurrection. The initial reaction to the message "He has been raised" is not joy, but puzzlement and confusion. The memories of death are still too fresh and vivid to be swept aside by the message. And what does the message mean anyway? They do not see Jesus. He is gone.

The women of the resurrection open up for us new perspectives on a spirituality of the resurrection and a ministry of reconciliation. It will be worthwhile to reflect upon women's roles in reconciliation. The tomb story focuses especially on death and on the experience of absence and abyss faced by those still suffering the shock of violence and death. That, too, will bear some reflection on our part. From this will emerge a first sketch of what the resurrection means for shaping a spirituality and a ministry of reconciliation.

Women and Reconciliation

One of the central facts that must be faced in a ministry of reconciliation is that men are most frequently the source of the violence that rends families, communities, and nations apart. Some account for this by noting that males are more aggressive physically than are females, and that this goes back to our distant past when the man's strength was needed to defend women and children from harm. Whether aggression is in the genes or whether it is learned behavior remains a matter of debate. However, it always leaves human wreckage strewn in its wake.

The other side of this fact is that it is often left to women to find ways of repairing the damage that men's violence and conflict have wrought. Sometimes they are the survivors; the men are no longer there. At other times women are the ones who are able to imagine alternatives that break the deadlock of a conflictive situation.

The stories that could be cited are many. Two that have recently come out of South Africa exemplify both being a survivor and finding an alternative. Both occurred in 1996 during the early sessions of the Truth and Reconciliation Commission. Modeled on reconciliation efforts in Chile, these forums were set up so that survivors could speak of the violations of human rights that had been perpetrated and wrongdoers could admit to and confess their offenses in order to be given amnesty. One of the first women who came forward told the story of being forced to watch her son's execution. She was not allowed to say good-bye to him, nor was she allowed to claim his body. At this point, all she wanted to know was where he had been buried.

The parallel to another woman who witnessed her son's execution immediately springs to mind. In John's gospel we hear that Mary, the mother of Jesus, was present at her son's execution (Jn 19:25-27). It is almost impossible to imagine a mother watching such a terrible thing. Yet this shocking scene has occurred again and again in our history.

Another woman came forward to the Truth and Reconciliation Commission to describe how her son had been taken away from her home, tortured, and killed; she told the Commission that his body had been returned to her. When asked by the presiding officer what she wanted from the new government, she paused a moment and then said, "I want the government to buy a tombstone for my son." She did not ask for justice for her son, only a tombstone. Reconciliation had touched her heart, and she did not seek revenge. She only wanted an acknowledgment on the part of the new government of what the apartheid government had done.

The stories of women protesting against violence and organizing to combat violence in a non-violent way are many.[1] One of the most powerful is the story of the Mothers of the Plaza de Mayo, who began gathering in that square in the heart of Buenos Aires in 1977 to protest the disappearance of their loved ones. They would march in circles, their heads covered with handkerchiefs. The government tried to break up the group of women, and to intimidate them. At one point, the police arrested nine of them, including one of their leaders, Azucena Villaflor. Two of those who were arrested were French nuns, who were tortured and then murdered (thrown from a helicopter into the sea, a favorite method of execution by the government at that time). Villaflor remains among the disappeared.

By 1982, the Mothers had grown to a group of 2,500 women. Their protest was pivotal in the downfall of the government. Their gathering in that plaza in the heart of Buenos Aires is an example of what Bronkhorst calls the genesis phase of transition. They were in many ways the symbolic event that marked the turning of the tide in what has become known as the "dirty war" (*guerra sucia*). A small number of the Mothers continue to march in their circle in the Plaza de Mayo on Thursdays to this day, protesting the disappearance of loved ones. Their slogan: "They were taken alive: Where are they?"

One thinks too of the mothers in southern shantytowns of Lima in the 1980s who banded together to feed the children in the *comedores populares* (community kitchens). They were perceived as a major threat by the *sendero luminoso* (Shining Path) guerrillas. The *senderistas* were bent on destroying any beneficent agency in Peruvian society so as to provoke their Maoist revolution. They also attacked gender roles of care and kindness, recruiting women to stage executions in the villages in

---

[1]For a sampling of those stories, see Daan Bronkhorst, *Truth and Reconciliation: Obstacles and Opportunities for Human Rights* (Amsterdam: Amnesty International, 1995), 107-117.

the Andes highlands. The women of the *comedores populares* presented an opposing image of care for the community. Despite intimidation and violence perpetrated against them, the women continued.

Another group was the women of the Wall of Peace in Croatia. When Serbs invaded and took over parts of Croatia in the Balkan War in 1991, one of their techniques of terror was the rape of women. When Croatian troops retook the area some years later, Croatian women went ahead of the troops and moved into the homes of the women in the Serbian villages. They would not allow the troops to rape the Serbian women in revenge for what had been done to Croatian women. They formed what they called the "wall of peace."

Women are often the victims of the violence in a special way because of patriarchy. One visitor to the Rwandan refugee camp in Bukavu in 1995 remarked on how few women were there. He was told that most of them had never reached the camp. They had drowned while trying to cross the Ruzizi River when escaping Rwanda. Women were not taught to swim, so when they tried to cross the river, they perished while the men survived.[2]

And then there are women like Yessie Macchi in Uruguay, who runs the *Centro mujer y memoria* (Center for Women and Memory), a documentation center about women who have been imprisoned for their political convictions. Her account of being released from prison reminds us that women not only suffer from violence, but their suffering is different from that of men:

> Being a woman of forty and coming out of prison is very different than when a man of forty is released. We all have to cope with a world that's changed enormously. We have to get used to the fact that we can walk more than a few metres; our health is considerably worse. Often your eyes need to adjust to seeing at a distance. All things you've forgotten in prison. Men have

---

[2] I owe this account to Richard Bliese, of the Chicago Center for Global Ministries.

a wife or family waiting for them. But a woman has to take care of her family when she's released.[3]

What all of these stories point to is the pivotal role women play in suffering, violence, and reconciliation. They are frequently the victims. They are the ones left behind to reconstruct a new society. They are the ones who survive. And they are the ones who find a non-violent way out of violent situations. They teach others how to cope, to heal memories, and to move on.

Perhaps that is why Jesus appeared first to women: they are the ones who most frequently lead acts of reconciliation that can come to make a difference. They are the ambassadors of reconciliation par excellence. Nils Christie, in his work of creating reconciliation circles for prisoners in the penitentiaries in Norway, contrasts the biblical image of Moses the lawgiver, delivering decrees from on high, with that of the women at the well, who gather to share their stories and work out together ways to respond creatively despite their constraints.[4] Christie uses this analogy to help male prisoners develop circles of reconciliation that can help them come to terms with their pasts.

All of this points to an important dimension of a spirituality of reconciliation. A spirituality of reconciliation involves not directing one's thinking along the traditional channels of power, but making possible the springing up of alternatives to dominative power. To counter power with the same kind of power may restrain it, but it does not lead to peace. This is something practitioners of non-violence have known for a long time. But it is a lesson hard to learn. The power that broke the hold of sin on the world was the powerlessness, the agony, and the humiliation of the cross. The blood that was shed in violence becomes life-giving, redeeming blood. Reconciliation requires finding a different kind of power from dominative power to transform situations. Matthilde Mellibovsky, one of

[3]Bronkhorst, op. cit., 108.

[4]Reported in Jakob Arnbjerg, "Is There Room for Reconciliation in the Penal System?" *Reconciliation on the Way to Graz 1997* (Copenhagen: Church of Denmark Council on Inter-Church Relations and the Ecumenical Council of Denmark, 1997).

the Mothers of the Plaza de Mayo, speaks of it as a "circle of love around death." The women in Croatia called it a wall of peace. It is the power that raised Jesus from the dead.

Women, and women's experience, are essential to the spirituality and the ministry of reconciliation. Women's endless experience of domination by men in cultures of patriarchy has been a school for thinking about alternatives, for seeing a different way. Since a ministry of reconciliation requires seeing a different way, part of creating communities of reconciliation is the cultivation of ways of living together outside the usual paths of power and domination.

What did the women see at the tomb where Jesus had been laid? The tomb stories tell us that they experienced confusion, puzzlement, even fear. Mary Magdalene, in John's gospel account, met Jesus and did not recognize him. What does all of this say?

I think it tells us that resurrection is not something we expect or can anticipate. The resurrection of Jesus was unprecedented in human history; there is no analogous event with which to compare it. When people spoke of the resurrection at the time of Jesus, they imagined it to be something like the resuscitation of the dead. Even in the subsequent centuries of Christianity, a very physicalist understanding of resurrection has prevailed. The appearance stories make it clear that resurrection is more than that. Jesus had been so transformed that initially even his closest disciples did not recognize him. Mary Magdalene thought he was the caretaker. The two disciples on the road to Emmaus walked with him for a long time and did not recognize him. The disciples in the upper room thought he was some ghost who had come to haunt them. The resurrection comes as a surprise.

Moments when reconciliation occurs are moments of surprise, like the experience of encountering the risen Lord in the appearance stories. As was noted in the last chapter, reconciliation always takes us to a new place. It does not simply transport us back to where we had been before the trauma occurred. Those who have experienced reconciliation or work with those seeking it know how difficult it is to imagine an alternative, to be prepared for a surprise. Before they happen, alternatives and surprises seem not to honor the terror and the pain of the experience of violence. Yet what keeps people trapped in the memories of violence is precisely the dilemma of integrating the traumatic experience into their identity, on the one hand, and escaping its grasp, on the other. This is something to which we will return in later chapters.

With the surprise in the resurrection appearance stories comes recognition. In Mark's account, there is no recognition. The women leave and do not speak to anyone. In John's account of this appearance (Jn 20:1-18), Mary Magdalene comes to recognize that the one she mistook for the caretaker is Jesus. Jesus speaks her name and she recognizes him. "Rabbouni!" (teacher), she cries.

Recognition is the turning point in the surprise, when the grace of reconciliation rushes into our hearts. It is the moment when the surprise connects with the experience and allows the experience to illumine and transform us. Often that recognition, however, comes to us in stages. In John's account of Peter and the Beloved Disciple entering the tomb, the Beloved Disciple "believes," but still does not understand the meaning (Jn 20:8-9). Recognition in its first stage is knowing that one has been brought to a new place, but not yet knowing clearly what that place is. Perhaps that is why Jesus tells Mary not to touch him, because she does not yet understand their changed relationship. He is indeed Jesus, but now in another and new way.

So too the experience of reconciliation. One can sense that one is in a new place, but realize that it is still uncharted territory. Sometimes that new territory is explored as a vocation, a calling to heal others. Sometimes it becomes the project of a lifetime. This is a theme to which we will return. Now it is time to examine more closely that space of confusion in the story. It is the space of the tomb.

Tomb and Absence

The puzzlement, confusion, and fear that the women experience in Mark's account, and the disorientation of Mary Magdalene in John's account reveal a tangled web of emotions and thoughts. The trauma of the execution of Jesus is still fresh in their minds. His burial had been hasty. And now nothing is as it should be: a shock upon a shock. The tomb is open. The body is gone. It is like being thrown off balance by shifting sand. There is no orientation point from which to regain equilibrium. Let us see if we can untangle some of the elements in the story, so as to trace the experience of the survivors of this trauma.

First of all, there is the tomb itself, which was to have served as an anchor in the stormy seas of emotion that surrounded Jesus' violent death. Even though Jesus had been taken away from them, the tomb was a place where the women could come to give focus to their feelings of loss. But now the tomb itself has been violated. The stone has been rolled back and the body is gone. It is empty. Rather than being a place where they can focus their feelings and mourn their loss, the tomb has become a sign of absence.

Knowing where the dead are is important to the survivors. This is especially the case when death has been violent, and even more so when people have "disappeared." This word took on a frightening new meaning in Latin America in the 1970s and thereafter, when it came to mean being kidnapped by the police or the army. The kidnapping was frequently followed by torture and death. Sometimes the body was deposited in a public place as a warning to others. Sometimes the body was never found, having been interred in an undisclosed place.

It is hard to imagine the pain this causes to the survivors of the disappeared. It is caught in Mary Magdalene's plaintive cry, "They have taken away my Lord, and I do not know where they have laid him" (Jn 20:13). Her cry is the cry of mothers, daughters, and friends of the disappeared around the world today. It is the cry of the Mothers of the Plaza de Mayo: "They were taken away alive: Where are they?" Here are voices from the families of the disappeared in Chile:

- "My wound had to heal without first being cleansed. I know he was killed, but they never returned his body to me. The mourning period is still going on."

- "Every time I see a madman or a hobo in the street I think it may be my husband; or that he might be somewhere in a similar condition."
- "Until recently we hoped to find them alive. Today we are going around looking for the bones. This is never going to end... this long nightmare from which I don't know if I can wake up, because I've forgotten what it means to live a normal life."[5]

Disappearance opens up a special kind of absence. It is an absence caused by uncertainty, in which the imagination runs wild, churning out all kinds of possibilities about where the disappeared might be. It generates questions about the condition of the disappeared, or how they died. But there is only silence: there is no one to answer the questions. Disappearance completely disorients the survivors: "I've forgotten what it means to live a normal life." The absence caused by a normal death is at least focused by burial. One has a place to which one can go and begin to work through the feelings of loss. Or, as South African Zbigniew Herbert has put it, "ignorance about the disappeared undermines the reality of the world."[6]

Since the experience of reconciliation efforts in Chile, the world now knows how important it is to identify the disappeared and the dead, to open common graves, and to accord the dead an honorable burial. In Chile after the dictatorship, the Truth and Reconciliation Commission set about identifying who had been killed and the circumstances under which each killing had taken place. Efforts were made around the country to locate the mass graves into which the arrested and disappeared had been dumped, to identify the remains, and to rebury them with the care and love that restored in some measure the dignity of the dead. A memorial has been set up in the municipal cemetery in Santiago listing the names of those who disappeared but whose remains have not been found. Here

---

[5] *Report of the Chilean National Commission on Truth and Reconciliation.* Tr. Phillip E. Berryman (Notre Dame, IN: University of Notre Dame Press, 1993), vol. II, 780-782.

[6] In Alex Boraine, Janet Levy, and Ronell Scheffer (eds.), *Dealing with the Past: Truth and Reconciliation in South Africa* (Capetown: IDASA, 1994), 58.

loved ones can come to mourn those who lie buried at some unknown location.

Since that experience in Chile, other countries have undertaken the same process of identifying the victims of human rights violations and locating the remains of those who have not been accorded a proper burial. In El Salvador, in Bosnia, and in other sites of these violations a grieving people open mass graves in order to bring closure to a violent past.

Jesus' body had been interred, but the rites that mark death and burial had been denied him. That was what the women had come to do. Encountering an open tomb and the absence of the body violated both them and the dead Jesus. By anointing his body and wrapping him in a proper shroud, they could acknowledge their loss of him and initiate a new relationship to him in memory. Not being able to do this foreclosed the possibility of that new relation. This was a violation of them in their relationship to Jesus. That Jesus' body appeared to have been taken away was the final insult after the humiliation and suffering of the execution.

An empty tomb confronts us with a yawning abyss of absence. It is not absence in the sense of a lack of presence. Rather, it is an absence that threatens to swallow us up in nothingness, to annihilate our own existence. One way of understanding that absence is by comparing it with those black holes which astronomers tell us are in outer space. They are dense concentrations of matter that swallow up and annihilate anything that comes close to them. Even light, which illumines darkness, disappears into the black hole. The absence the women felt at the empty tomb was like a black hole, threatening to swallow them as it had swallowed Jesus in death. That would help account somewhat for the mixture of confusion and fear they were experiencing.

This terrible absence is, like a black hole, not simply a passive emptiness waiting to be filled. It is a menacing awareness of a force that is fundamentally set against all that exists and is good. This absence is the experience of evil, what St. Augustine called many centuries ago the *privatio boni*, the absence of the good. Survivors of torture have expressed the experience of this special kind of absence. Devout Christians have recounted how, in the midst of their torture, they did not feel the presence of God, even though they knew that God sides with the oppressed. No, they did not feel that presence at all. All that they did experience was this menacing absence. Perhaps the women at the tomb that day experienced such a thing.

The terrible absence experienced at the tomb, the absence experienced in traumatic events such as torture, point to why reconciliation is so difficult and efforts to achieve it are often not successful. Reconciliation is not just about getting things back to where they used to be, or getting back to normal living. It is struggling with evil and the consequences of evil itself. The absence swallows the good and spews forth lies in its place. It is an absence which, when questioned, hums with a numbing, deadening silence. It is with this that efforts of reconciliation must contend, because that terrible absence threatens every form of life and flourishing. We cannot allow that absence to engulf the world.

That is why establishing a focus for grief is so important. That is why we establish memorial monuments for the dead. That is why the woman in South Africa wanted the new government to provide a tombstone for her son. We must have a secure place where we can interact with the dead, where we can engage in those rituals that reestablish our own shaky footing in an unstable world. The tomb gives us something to hold on to lest we be sucked into the vortex of absence.

The absence of the body from the tomb breaks again the relationship that burial tried to establish. Death is always a rupture of relationships, and grieving and mourning are a way of trying to reestablish relationships, albeit now in a different way. This is portrayed in a poignant fashion in John's account of Mary recognizing that the stranger is Jesus. Jesus tells her not to cling to him—"Do not hold on to me." One cannot hold on to the dead; a new kind of relationship has to be established. Much of what Jesus does in the healing stories that will be explored in the following chapters is to shape new kinds of relationships with his disciples. The most important relationship of presence to combat absence will be in the Eucharist.

Remaking relationships is an important part of the reconciliation process. What often makes the readjustment process after transforming change so unsatisfying is that old relationships have not been allowed to change. One of the struggles in South Africa today, for example, has to do with moving from a posture of resistance to one of reconstruction. How do you move from struggling against a great evil to collaborating in order to create a just society? The process mobilizes a different set of emotions and calls for compromises. It is perhaps for this reason that reconciliation is so difficult to attain.

Out of the absence in the tomb flow other memories. Part of the feeling of entanglement that the women experienced at the tomb—and that people feel in the face of evil during the reconciliation process—is that other memories are uncovered as well. Some of these memories are repressed ones that have been too painful to deal with. Others are ones that we thought had lost any significance for us and so have been forgotten. All kinds of things come to the surface that we thought we had long buried. Some of the emotions that come with the memories—emotions of anger, loss, and fear—have become detached from the original events that had generated them, and now roam around our lives like lost spirits.

In the months and years of a reconciliation process, those roaming emotions will continue to seep out. This is especially true of emotions that were engendered by trauma. A sound, a chance encounter in the street, a distinctive smell can set off anew a paroxysm of feeling. What becomes apparent is that we need more than just a tomb to give them focus, we also need a safe place for memory to be revisited and sorted out. Reconciliation processes try to create new spaces that are safe for revisiting the experience of trauma. Those safe places are not easily created. As we shall see in chapter 4 when we look at the story of the disciples in the upper room, they were looking for such a safe place, and were stunned when Jesus walked right through all their barricaded security. In the next chapter, on the Emmaus story, we will watch how the Stranger helps the two disciples untangle their memories and reweave them into a new story.

Events may pass, but memories linger. Memories of traumatic events can become enshrouded in emotions so strong that we can no longer penetrate to the memories themselves. In the tangle of their emotions, the three women hastened away from the tomb. The last words of the original ending of the story are: "for they were afraid."

The Tomb and the Spirituality of Reconciliation

We turn in conclusion to sketch preliminarily what the experience of the empty tomb can teach us about the spirituality of reconciliation.

Women are the first witnesses to the resurrection. It is the women, who count for little in society at that time, who are given the first news of what God has done to their executed master and teacher. In spite of their confusion and amazement, they are the first to understand, even though the male disciples do not believe them (cf. Mk 16:10-11; Lk 24:10-11). The spirituality that sustains reconciliation parallels in many ways women's experience of being pushed to the margins and not taken seriously. It is a spirituality that is not built up by the exercise of dominative power. Its power is not Moses on the mountain; it is women at the well. It is a spirituality that can see with different eyes, that can see what the women saw. Were reconciliation a return of things to their condition previous to the trauma and violation, ordinary dominative power would be sufficient. But because reconciliation takes us to a new place, dominative power cannot engineer the solution. Counterviolence cannot end violence; it can only perpetuate it in a new form. The search for non-violent alternatives and imagining a different future are activities of this spirituality. This quest and this creativity create the space for surprises to happen—and the moment of reconciliation comes upon us as a surprise. To be locked into a certain way of thinking and feeling precludes recognition of the graced event of reconciliation when it does come.

A spirituality of reconciliation deals with various forms of absence. It deals with loss, with losing someone or something that can never be retrieved. It works to set up new relations, relations that acknowledge that the loved one cannot return, but that some kind of relationship is still possible. But first the loss must be acknowledged, and the skein of emotions that surrounds the loss—anger, fear, uncertainty, betrayal—must be untangled and rendered less virulent.

A spirituality of reconciliation deals with dislocation, with the disorientation that is caused by traumatic experience. It wanders with the victim through the ruined territory, looking for bits and pieces of a shattered life, looking for those who have disappeared. "They have taken away my Lord, and I do not know where they have laid him." A spirituality of reconciliation collects the shards of a shattered existence carefully, and helps the victims piece them back together as best they can. It goes in search of those who have disappeared.

It struggles to deal with the abyss, that terrible black hole that is the space of evil, that absence that swallows all being and even light. This is the most awesome of the forms of absence, one that feeds upon the living and makes the possibility of any reconciliation often seem forever beyond reach. The spiritual strength needed to deal with this absence requires a steadfastness of faith, a rock-like sense of trust, and a firm hope that things will be otherwise. Here, facing the abyss, we come as close as we can to grasping the enormity and the complexity of what reconciliation will entail. Here we feel the traumas of the past most keenly as they are made frighteningly present to us once again. Here we face the challenge of acknowledging what that past has done to us. And here we face the challenges of honoring what we have become because of the past, and transcending that past so that its grip upon us will not control our lives.

It is at this moment in a spirituality of reconciliation, of struggling with the abyss, that we have perhaps the best opportunity to understand the meaning of Jesus' death as sacrifice. The language of sacrifice is incomprehensible to many people today. It sounds to them as though God were an abusive father, demanding the death of his son. It sounds like the perpetuation of violence rather than any cessation of it.

Sacrifice is a notoriously hard concept to understand. Indeed, it is not a univocal concept, but is a name used for a variety of actions that attempt communication between the human and the divine or transcendent spheres.[7] Contemplation of the abyss reveals the enormity and complexity of the evil that has been perpetrated upon a society. What would it take to overcome it? The images of cross and blood figure prominently in the Pauline language of reconciliation (cf. Rom 5:9; Col 1:20; Eph 2:13-16). Both cross and blood have paradoxical meanings that allow them to bridge the distance between the divine and human worlds, between life and death. The cross was the ultimate sign of Roman power over a conquered and colonized people. To be crucified was the most dishonorable and humiliating of ways to die. The cross stood as a sign of reassertion of Roman power and the capacity to reject and exclude utterly. Yet it was through the crucified Christ that God chose to reconcile the world. The apparent triumph of worldly power is turned against itself and becomes "Christ the power of God and the wisdom of God" (1 Cor 1:24). For John, the cross is at once instrument of humiliation and Christ's throne of glory (Jn 12:32). Similarly, blood is a sign of the divine life that God has breathed into every living being, and its shedding is a sign of death. The blood of the cross (Col 1:20) becomes the means of reconciling all things to God. In its being shed, the symbol of violence and death becomes the symbol of reconciliation and peace. To understand sacrifice, one must be prepared to inhabit the space within these paradoxes. Sacrifice understood in this way is not about the abuse of power, but about a transformation of power.

A spirituality of reconciliation can be deepened by a meditation on the stories of the women and the tomb. These stories invite us to place inside them our experience of marginalization, of being incapable of imagining a way out of a traumatic past, of dealing with the kinds of absence that traumas create. They invite us to let the light of the resurrection—a light that even the abyss cannot extinguish—penetrate those absences.

---

[7]Robert Schreiter, *In Water and in Blood: A Spirituality of Solidarity and Hope* (New York: Crossroad, 1988), 11-13, is the basis for the explanation given here.

CHAPTER 3

"We Had Hoped That He Was the One to Redeem Israel"

(Luke 24:13-35)

A Story of Coming to Faith

The story of the disciples on the road to Emmaus is one of the most cherished of the appearance stories. The touching account of how Jesus journeys alongside two dispirited and disappointed disciples and slowly touches their hearts and opens their eyes has been a source of inspiration and hope for generations of believers. His sitting at table with the disciples in Emmaus has inspired many artistic portrayals of that moment when he is recognized in the breaking of the bread (Lk 24:31). It is a story with many layers of meaning. It models a way of leading that is a walking alongside; it examines change of perspective; it celebrates coming to faith.

In this chapter we wish to look closely at this remarkable story to see what clues it yields for understanding the resurrection and a spirituality of reconciliation. The Emmaus story, as we shall see, is one of the best stories into which many of us can place our own story and other stories of reconciliation. In order to do that, we will begin by recounting the story, calling to attention specific elements that deserve special scrutiny, and then turn to reflect on some of the themes that the story raises.

The story begins on that same first day of the week when the women had their experience at the tomb of Jesus. Two disciples of Jesus leave Jerusalem and head out in the direction of the village of Emmaus. The story unfolds in their journey of about seven miles to that village.

All along the way they are talking intensely with each other about what has just happened to them. At one point they are overtaken by a stranger, someone whom they do not recognize. He asks them what it is that they are discussing. They are surprised that he does not know what has been going on in Jerusalem during the last few days. He asks, "What things?" They then recount what has happened, telling him about Jesus "who was a prophet mighty in deed and word before God and all the people," who ran afoul of the religious authorities, and who was crucified. They end the story of Jesus with their disappointed plaint, "But we had hoped that he was the one to redeem Israel." That hope is now very much something of the past. And then they turn to the remarkable reports from the women at the tomb, which leave them even more confused.

The stranger admonishes them for not understanding, and affirms that this Jesus was indeed the one who would save Israel. His death was necessary for him to enter into his glory. Then, as they continue along their way, the stranger retells for them the whole story of Israel from the perspective of their crucified leader. The words of the stranger are having a remarkable effect. Their hearts are burning within them, and they find their hope coming back.

They near the village, and the stranger appears to be continuing on. They spontaneously urge him to stay with them for the evening, for night is falling. The stranger agrees to do so. As they recline at table to eat together, the stranger blesses and breaks the bread and, all at once, their eyes are opened. This stranger is none other than Jesus himself! But just as they recognize him, he vanishes from their sight. After spending some moments in astonishment, recounting to each other how deeply they have been touched, they get up immediately from the table and hasten back to Jerusalem to tell the others what (or better, whom) they have seen.

Let us turn now to attend closely to some elements of the story that reveal for us both the meaning of the resurrection and the process and spirituality of reconciliation.

The Journey

The journey is one of Luke's favorite themes, and it provides a structure for much of the gospel, particularly after Jesus "sets his face to go to Jerusalem" in Luke 9:51. The journey on which the two disciples set out is unclear in many ways. Are they going to Emmaus, or are they merely escaping Jerusalem? It seems to be more the latter than the former since, after they have seen the Lord, they appear not even to finish their meal, let alone do whatever may have brought them to Emmaus in the first place. It is likely, then, that the journey for the two disciples was more a trying to get away from something than a trying to get somewhere.

The journeys we make toward reconciliation often seem like the disciples' journey to Emmaus. We are mostly trying to flee the pain of the past and really do not know where we are heading except that it is someplace away from where we now are. The result is that the journey becomes tedious and burdensome in itself as we seem to "get nowhere" even though we are moving all the time. If we knew where we had to go to escape all of this, we would gladly do so. But no clear route presents itself. It is like being trapped on a treadmill that keeps us moving but never takes us anywhere.

Overcoming the past is often such an experience. The memories and the nightmares recur and, despite the passage of time, remain as vivid and uncontrollable as ever. We seem stuck and unable to maneuver to a better place or perspective. We need to find someone to accompany us, someone who will give us guidance.

Jesus appears in the story as someone who overtakes the disciples on the road and falls in with them, accompanying them on their journey. This act of accompanying the disciples is a powerful image that can become a model for our own pastoral praxis. We do not walk ahead of people so much as alongside them, speaking with them, hearing their stories, comforting them, challenging them when necessary.

Many of us need this kind of accompaniment on our journeys to reconciliation. Those who accompany us may not be able to provide the definitive interpretation of our burdens, but they can become a means by which those burdens are lifted. They can create an atmosphere of safety and trust that makes possible our finding the way out of our distress.

The Story

As the disciples walk, they are involved in an intense interchange, so much so that they do not even see the stranger approaching. Such intensity reveals something of their emotional state. To speak that intensely about a recent experience means that it must carry great importance, but no clear meaning and direction for the people involved. They have to keep retelling the story so as to integrate it into the story of their own lives.

But the story is not coming together for them. The story of Jesus, with its disappointing end, has now become burdensome. In verses 19 and 20, the disciples actually get the story of Jesus right: he was a prophet mighty in deed and word before God and all the people. This phrase could be a confession of faith in Jesus, but for these disciples it is not. They have the words right, but it is not liberating for them.

This is the experience of many who deal with a painful past. They can get all the words right, but something still is missing. It still does not all come together. In the Emmaus story in Luke, what was missing was faith. In our own struggle toward reconciliation, what is missing is often not that clear. We struggle to find the one thing that will help us overcome the pain, transform the memory, allow us to get on with our lives. But it just does not seem to come. The struggle to find the way to interpret our story is frequently a gradual retelling of that story until it becomes a new story.

One possible key to why the story kept being a burden rather than a pathway out of suffering can be found in the words of verse 21: "We had hoped that he was the one to redeem Israel." It was a hope whose light had been extinguished. When hope is lost, it is hard to find the way out. One becomes a kind of lost soul, wandering without destination, condemned to keep moving but never to arrive. The same formulae repeat themselves, the same stories are told, but nothing ever changes and the burden never becomes lighter.

The stranger provides the key, although at the time the disciples fail to get the point. The point is that the death of Jesus is not the end of the story, but a key transition to allow the story to come to its genuine fulfillment. To help them get the point, the stranger retells not only the Jesus story, but also the whole long story of God's action in the world. The hearts of the disciples are beginning to stir. Perhaps they will begin to understand.

In retelling the story, Jesus provides a shift of perspective. The story is already familiar to the disciples, but now they are hearing it from a different perspective. They had thought that the shameful death of Jesus meant that Jesus was not the mighty one of God after all, that he had been abandoned or even rejected by God. But that death, as the stranger now tells it, is the turning point in the story. It allows the mighty prophet of God to make the transition from this world into the realm of glory, showing that he truly is the Messiah, the one whom God has sent.

If you listen to people who have come to reconciliation, survivors whose humanity has been restored after human rights violations, this shift in perspective is always an important turning point. It reorients their story without diminishing the gravity of what has happened. Frequently, what is revealed, as the stranger reveals it in the Jesus story, is that the most painful and degrading part of the burden they carry turns out to be more than pure evil or utter absence such as the women experienced at the tomb. The burden reveals a purpose that reorients perspective, a calling to move in a different direction, or a commission to undertake some task. This in no way trivializes the experience that the survivor had gone through. It does take away its demonic power over the survivor's life. The energy that swirled around the story can be directed to some purpose, rather than feeding on itself like a growing hurricane.

What happens in the telling and retelling of the story is the healing of memory. So much of our identity is tied up with memory. This becomes more and more apparent the older we get, when the greater part of our life lies behind us rather than ahead of us. The memory of persons and events important to us is stored in narratives. As our circumstances change, our sense of those narratives changes: we recall elements that we thought we had forgotten, or find a different perspective from which to view the narrative.

Memories of trauma—the loss of a loved one, the experience of betrayal, the violation of basic human rights—become centers of pain that paralyze everything around them. We find ourselves drawn back to the memories to relive the anguish and suffering. Indeed, we seem unable to escape them. Such is the case with the disciples on the road to Emmaus. They are trying to escape Jerusalem and the terrible memory of the death of Jesus, but the story accompanies them on the road. They keep repeating it over and over again. Even when they have the words right, the emotional intensity of the experience will not allow them to hear the story from a different perspective. It takes the insight of the stranger to pry them loose from that interpretation. Once a new perspective is gained on a particularly traumatic experience, the story must be retold—and not only that story, but many other stories as well. We see this in the Emmaus story: the stranger not only retells the story of Jesus, but has to recast the whole story of God's dealing with Israel as well. In our dealing with the retelling of a story of trauma, the retelling of all the stories with which it connects can become the work of a lifetime.

Even then, the pain never entirely disappears from the story of trauma. It can flare up again unexpectedly, triggered by a random event. In the case of human rights abuses, unknown reserves of pain and anger well up again when new information comes to light. The experiences that have grown out of Truth and Reconciliation Commissions in Chile, El Salvador, and South Africa have made this abundantly clear. When a concrete name or face is attached to a heinous act, it is as though the memory was never in any way healed. The victim is put through the same roller coaster of emotion all over again.

A concrete example of the healing of memory might help here. I remember hearing a story from a woman a number of years ago about the death of her son. She and her husband had had to wait a long time for the birth of their only child. He grew up to be an extraordinary young man. He was outgoing and generous, involved in social justice programs, and much loved by all those who knew him. In the summer holidays after his first year at university, he was killed in a construction accident at the site where he was working. His parents were utterly devastated. The message of eternal life in Christ brought no comfort to them. They stopped seeing their friends and withdrew from their usual social activities. They could not bring themselves to part with his belongings; they kept his room exactly as it had been that day when he left for work and never came home. This continued for over a year, as they recounted for themselves over and over again his death and what might have been done to prevent it. And then one day, all of a sudden, something changed. His mother realized that their son had always been actively engaged in other peoples' lives, caring for them and being of assistance in any way he could. He would not have wanted them—his parents—closing themselves off in this way. That was not what *he* would have done. The realization of that lifted much of the burden from her. She shared her insight with her husband, who grasped it immediately. They threw themselves into all kinds of activity in their parish, because they knew that this was what their son would have had them do. They still miss him terribly, but they are consoled in the fact that they are doing what he would have wanted them to do.

The story had been retold from another perspective—and it made all the difference. The couple had always known of the selflessness of their son, but it had never before meant to them what it did in that moment.

In the reconciliation process, these are the moments of grace. For the disciples on the road to Emmaus, that moment of grace came gradually. Their hearts first began to stir, and then to burn as they heard the story retold. But ultimately the change came not even from the retelling of the story, but from something the stranger did—how he blessed and broke bread. Only then were their eyes opened.

How long or how often must a story be retold before it turns into a redemptive story rather than a burdensome, oppressive one? No one can ever know for sure. The moment of grace is precisely that—a moment of grace, when suddenly the perspective shifts, a new meaning is found, and a pathway appears, leading out of the deep tangle of memories, emotions, and stories of death.

Recognition in the Breaking of the Bread

The stranger's retelling of the story of Jesus and the story of Israel sets something stirring in the hearts of the disciples. It is still not all that clear, but the outlines are beginning to emerge. As they near the village of Emmaus, it appears that the stranger is going farther. Spontaneously, the disciples invite the stranger to stay with them for the night. The day is nearly over, but they do not want the marvelous exchange with the stranger to end. "Stay with us," they say. The disciples find themselves in a graced moment. And they want it to continue as long as possible.

They invite the stranger to eat with them. He joins them at table, and then it happens. He takes bread, blesses and breaks it, and gives it to them. Their eyes are opened. Now they recognize who the stranger is. It is none other than Jesus.

As they gasp in amazement, Jesus disappears. The disciples are left alone, holding the bread that Jesus has given them.

This remarkable scene in the story brims with meanings. It begins with the disciples' invitation to the stranger to stay with them and eat with them. Perhaps this is the first hint of the healing and reconciliation that is taking place. The disciples, so despondent on the road, now extend hospitality to the stranger. There is something about their humanity that has been restored, and they are now able to be more than passive listeners: they are able to take action on behalf of others. They have been drawn out of a kind of death and are able to help build the circle of love once again. This is a sign that something is happening.

The stranger takes them the final part of the way. By blessing, breaking, and sharing bread they make the connection. During his lifetime Jesus had often shown them what the reign of God would be like by gathering them together at table to eat and drink. Now, by doing the same thing, he heals them. It is interesting to see what is at work here. Through all of the words he had spoken to them on the road that afternoon, they had not been quite able to recognize him, although their hearts had begun to burn within them. It is the breaking of bread that brings the moment of recognition. Their eyes are opened and they can finally see.

This experience of the disciples of the risen Jesus is often the experience in the moment of reconciliation. What triggers the actual moment of reconciliation may appear to the outsider as something secondary or even trivial. But, for the person being healed, that action or word becomes a window onto the eternal. It brings together and sums up precisely what has happened in the long process of reconciliation. It is what will be shared with others again and again. To repeat that gesture or to say that word leads one again into the world of grace.

Jesus' role in all of this as the stranger reveals many things as well. If we take all the appearance stories together, we find Jesus doing a lot of different and sometimes contradictory things. He walks through doors, but then he eats broiled fish (cf. Lk 24:36, 43). He does not allow Mary Magdalene to touch him, but invites Thomas to do so (Jn 20:17, 27). It can be rather hard to harmonize these actions with one another. But to try to do that is to be the puzzled outsider who fails to grasp the significance of the word said or the gesture given. It simply misses what is going on. *Jesus appears as he needs to be seen.* The purpose of the appearances is not to make a point or to establish a fact. It is to heal, to reconcile. Each of Jesus' appearances—to Mary Magdalene, to the disciples on the road to Emmaus, to the disciples in the upper room, to the disciples on the seashore—is to reestablish a relationship, to confirm a bond of trust, to touch and heal a broken heart. The mode and manner of Jesus' appearances are shaped to the needs of those who come to recognize who he is. The fact that in every appearance story he is not recognized at first—Magdalene thinks he is the caretaker, the disciples on the Emmaus road take him for an outsider, the disciples in the upper room fear that he is a ghost come to haunt them—reveals the deep need for healing. Jesus orchestrates each opportunity to invite his closest disciples to recognize him.

That Jesus is unrecognized at the beginning of each of these stories indicates how much Jesus has changed and how much the disciples need to change. Through the experience of resurrection, God has brought Jesus to a new place. Resurrection is more than resuscitation; it is a transformation, a transfiguration. There is continuity in Jesus' identity between his earthly life and his resurrected state. But he is truly transfigured, given a new form. The disciples will have to learn to see in a new way if they are to recognize Jesus. As Rowan Williams has put it, Easter "occurs when we find in Jesus not a dead friend, but a living stranger."[1]

Jesus has changed, but it is the disciples who still need to change. Jesus as stranger is the future they cannot recognize. Over and over again, the healing of the hearts is called in these stories "believing" or coming to faith. They must see Jesus—and themselves—with new eyes.

Believing or coming to faith is at once a gift from God, and accepting that gift requires from us an act of trust. Trust, the risk of believing in another, is fundamental to human life itself. The trust that is called forth by God connects us to God, and also humanizes us more deeply and more fully. We become self-extending to others, just as God has been to us.

It is this coming to faith that makes it possible to read the resurrection appearance stories as stories of reconciliation. For at the heart of reconciliation the victim has the same experience: receiving a gift that restores the victim's humanity, and makes it possible to trust again.

Recognizing Jesus, then, is more than acknowledging his presence. It is an experience of transformation. The moment of the breaking of the bread in Emmaus is a good example. Earlier in Luke's gospel, at the Last Supper, Jesus announces that he will not eat together with them again until the reign of God comes (22:15). The fact that Jesus breaks bread with them at Emmaus means that the reign of God has truly come. The disciples, in recognizing Jesus, are now truly in a different place. They are transformed, and set out immediately to go back to Jerusalem, hastening through the darkness to tell the other disciples what has happened to them.

The Emmaus Road and a Spirituality of Reconciliation

What lessons are to be learned about the resurrection and a spirituality of reconciliation from the Emmaus story? As we

---

[1]Rowan Williams, *Resurrection: Interpreting the Easter Gospel* (Harrisburg, PA: Morehouse Publishing, 1982), 82.

have seen, it is a rich and densely textured tale that touches upon human experience in so many different ways.

It is, first of all, paradigmatic of the resurrection experience. The women at the tomb in Mark's account are taken through only the first part of the experience. They encounter profound absence—the descent among the dead—and get only the slightest glimmer of what is to come. The disciples on the Emmaus road, however, are taken through the full experience. They begin downcast. As they make the journey out of Jerusalem to Emmaus, they journey also through their disillusionment and disappointment. "We *had* hoped that he would save Israel." But hope is gone. The stranger joins them and, ever so gently and gradually, helps them retell the story. The story retold begins to restore their humanity: they are able to offer hospitality to the stranger. The moment of recognition comes, and they are transformed. Filled with excitement and hope, and new purpose as well, they rush back to Jerusalem to share their newfound joy.

We can see different elements of a spirituality of reconciliation at work here. The stranger gains their trust and provides a safe place for them to tell their story. As they journey along the road, the stranger listens carefully and compassionately. The story gets retold until a new perspective emerges. The finding of the new perspective happens as a moment of grace that comes upon us. It is not something that we can construct for ourselves. It comes in a way that seems almost an afterthought to outsiders, but it is the window onto God's purposes for us, for the one being healed. Indeed, one could say that the perspective gained in the moment of reconciliation is the perspective that God takes. Or, as Rowan Williams has put it, "God is the agency that gives us back our memories, because God is the 'presence' to which all reality is present."[2] That is why it is such an empowering and joyful moment. We tremble in awe of what we now see.

In the Emmaus story, that is certainly what happens. Jesus recounts the whole biblical story from the perspective of God and what God wants for the world. Sometimes in reconciliation

---

[2] Ibid., 29.

stories such a God-centered perspective is not so evident. Sometimes what emerges appears to be the perspective of the loved one who has been lost—what we need to do is what he or she would have wanted. Think of the story recounted above of the couple who lost their son, and how they discovered healing in seeing themselves from the perspective from which he would have seen them. But, even in those cases, it is God speaking through the loved one. This becomes evident if we focus on what it is that the loved one would have wanted, or what the one needing healing is commissioned to do.

The stranger in the Emmaus story creates a circle of love in which the disciples can tell their story in safety and begin to rebuild trust. A zone of hospitality has been created. In that circle, memory can be gently unfolded and its wounds revealed. Memories make up a great part of our identity and our understanding of ourselves. In a circle of love those memories can be revisited in their pain and sorrow, not simply to relive the pain and sorrow, but to find a way to outlive them. It is in such a setting that the cup of suffering can be transformed into the cup of hope.

All of this moves the victim toward a new creation in which truth will reign. In the Emmaus story, the disciples had thought that the truth of the matter was that Jesus was not the one whom they had hoped would redeem Israel. But, in fact, he was. Coming to see the real truth helped them also to develop a praxis of doing the truth. Their offer of hospitality now to the stranger who, without their realizing, had been so hospitable to them, shows that they once again can live a life of truth. They are no longer beholden to the lie that the religious and civil authorities had tried to make of the mission of Jesus. They can live in the truth once again.

The Emmaus story is one of the best examples of how we can place our own stories in the bigger story of the passion, death, and resurrection of Jesus. It contains, too, the principal elements of a spirituality and ministry of reconciliation. No wonder it has been one of the favorite stories of Christians through the centuries.

CHAPTER 4

Peace, Forgiveness, and Food

(Luke 24:36-49; John 20:19-23)

The two accounts we have in Luke and John of the disciples huddled together in the upper room show us the followers of Jesus full of anxiety and fear. As has already been noted, at least the male disciples had every reason to be afraid. Their leader had been executed as an enemy of the state, and they stood to receive the same punishment if they were caught. To be fearful in this situation was to be realistic.

There were other reasons for being anxious and fearful as well. The disciples had abandoned Jesus to the temple guard, fleeing to save their own necks. Since none of them had been arrested, they hoped that now they were out of danger. But one could not be sure as yet. Even if they were safe, they felt guilty for having abandoned Jesus.

Peter's guilt was even deeper, since he had gone one step further by denying even knowing Jesus. The swaggering Peter, who had said that he would never desert Jesus, had now done precisely that. All of them, however, shared some of Peter's guilt. They had not stood by Jesus. God had not rescued him from the cross, so they did not know exactly what to believe about him now. Had he truly been God's Messiah, the Anointed One? Had the reign of God which he had promised really been true, since God appeared not to have come to save either Jesus or Israel? What had become of their Master and—now— what would become of them? What would Jesus say if he were to see them now?

"Peace Be with You"

Then it happens. Someone suddenly appears in the room, in their very midst. In Luke's account, they are startled and terrified, because they do not know who it is. Only a ghost can appear like that, walking through a locked door. What could a ghost want with them, sorry lot that they are? Is it perhaps the ghost of Jesus come back to haunt them for their lack of courage? Or the shade of Judas come to remind them that they in their faintheartedness are little different from him?

Unlike on the Emmaus road, here Jesus immediately identifies himself. Knowing that it is Jesus only complicates their feelings more. They rejoice to see him, but are also bewildered by all that is happening. They are also apprehensive. What will he say to them?

"Peace be with you." This is not exactly what they expect to hear, which is a reprimand, perhaps even a rebuke. The joy of seeing Jesus is commingled with guilt for what they have done—and especially for what they have not done. How can things ever be the same again?

What is going on in Jesus' mind at this point? He wants to assure them that it is truly he whom they are seeing. But what appears to be of most importance for him is to convey the experience of peace. The biblical idea of peace, of *shalom*, is a rich one. It means much more than the cessation of violence and conflict. It is the state in which the world is meant to be. It is the best description of what the reign of God will be like: a place of safety, justice, and truth; a place of trust, inclusion, and love; a place of joy, happiness, and well-being. The risen Jesus' very presence offers them that wonderful peace. For that is now the experience of Jesus. His suffering is behind him, and he now dwells in the peace of God.

What does it mean to experience peace after so much suffering? Only those who have suffered, those who carry around the memory of pain in their bodies, know how strong the yearning is for peace—and how far away peace can seem to be. Jesus had been tortured and then crucified. He had descended into the very maw of death. Piero della Francesca's painting of the risen Jesus captures this experience of suffering and then of death in the face—and especially in the eyes—of Jesus. The risen Jesus appears weary. There is a knowledge of sadness and absence in his eyes that has a haunting, ineffable quality.[1]

Those who have undergone great suffering know things that those who have not suffered can never know. But that great suffering of Jesus is now subsumed in the resurrection. Jesus now offers his disciples peace.

Is this peace the grace of reconciliation? The grace of reconciliation certainly flows from the resurrection. It is the experience of the "power of the resurrection" of which Paul speaks in Philippians 3:10. It is a restoration of humanity. Every experience of reconciliation is in some way an experience of this kind of peace, even when the peace, assuring as it may be, seems quite fragile. The peace that Jesus offers the disciples is a peace that has known suffering, and knows how costly peace can be.

If peace is the final state of reconciliation, it becomes important in reconciliation efforts to try to imagine what peace will look like. That picture will shift as the process moves along and, if reconciliation does take place, the final picture that does emerge will still come as a surprise. But the disciplined practice of imagining reconciliation is constructive because it keeps us focused on the goal. As the picture changes for us in the process, it also helps us see what is not part of reconciliation. Take, for example, how thinking about the final state of peace is imagined when justice is considered the goal of reconciliation. What happens in the process is that, first, it becomes clear that justice can mean many things. Justice initially means redress of wrongs (the pursuit of justice is sometimes even a covert way of taking revenge). This often leads to questions about just what kind of justice we are really seeking. Sometimes this is followed by reflecting on conditions for a just society. And we may end by realizing that it is truth—even more than justice—which we seek.

Imagining peace along the way, then, can be a way of disciplining our quest and keeping us focused on the ultimate goal. It frequently prepares us, too, for peace when peace does arrive.

---

[1]See the discussion in L. Gregory Jones, *Embodying Forgiveness: A Theological Analysis* (Grand Rapids, MI: Eerdmans, 1995), 300.

Forgiveness

In John's account of the appearance of Jesus in the upper room, the next theme that Jesus broaches is forgiveness. The disciples' first reaction may be to tense up: now Jesus is going to bring up the matter of their abandoning him! It would surely be appropriate, and might even ease some of the anguish that the disciples are feeling about their own guilt. But Jesus continues the theme of peace, and bestows on the disciples the capacity to forgive sins.

Forgiveness is one of the most thorny parts of the reconciliation process. We all know how hard it is to forgive when we have been hurt. We know too how hard it is to live up to the injunctions of Jesus to forgive seventy times seven and to love our enemies. The phrases in the Lord's Prayer that imply that divine forgiveness may hinge on our being able to forgive others ("forgive us our trespasses, as we forgive those who trespass against us") make forgiveness seem a duty that is sometimes impossible to perform. We know also how long it can take to forgive, and how animosities can even be passed down from one generation to the next. Is forgiveness really possible?

There is another aspect of forgiveness that makes it difficult. Forgiving can be seen as a betrayal of the past, and especially a betrayal of the dead. To forgive seems to wipe out the memory of what has happened. Forgiving can feel like negating a past that has changed the present and the future irrevocably. Simply to forgive is to pretend that all the pain never happened. Forgiving seems to be a way of punishing the victim once again, this time by erasing memory. The old adage "forgive and forget" cheapens, even trivializes, what has been a wrenching human experience.

Forgiving seems especially impossible in situations where the wrongdoer does not acknowledge what has been done. This is frequently the case after the end of civil conflict where the wrongdoers still remain in power or threaten to tip the delicate balance of peace if they are pressed in any uncomfortable direction. The anemic acknowledgement of wrongdoing put forth by former South African President F. W. De Klerk at the

Truth and Reconciliation Commission hearings probably angered far more South Africans than it satisfied. This also happens in face-to-face conflicts. The victim demands apology and repentance; the wrongdoer refuses to acknowledge any wrongdoing. This seems to stop any reconciliation in its tracks.

Forgiveness itself is a notoriously difficult task, and how it is undertaken varies somewhat from culture to culture.[2] Some cultures seem to be able to move into public forgiveness more easily than others. Here I wish to explore three aspects of this crucial, but often intractable, element of the reconciliation process that are pertinent to our reflections on resurrection and a spirituality of reconciliation. The first is divine and human forgiveness. The second has to do with where forgiveness fits in the process of reconciliation. The third is forgiving and forgetting.

Divine and Human Forgiveness

One of the most difficult things about forgiving someone involves grasping the enormity of the wrongdoing. That enormity often is greater than the act itself: it has consequences that move out in shock waves from the deed, reaching sometimes farther than we can see. Think, for example, about the different kinds of social conflict and oppression that so many countries have experienced in the twentieth century. Think of the genocides in Armenia and Cambodia, the Holocaust, the tyranny of Communist governments, the effects of imperialism on colonized peoples, the global wars, and the ethnic conflicts. The list goes on and on. How does one begin to forgive any of that? Even more personalized forms of wrongdoing may have consequences that cannot be grasped entirely. If someone has betrayed my trust, how can I begin to fathom the damage that has caused, and how can I begin to forgive and rebuild the relationship?

---

[2]See for one example, combining psychological and theological elements, Jean Monbourquette, "Processus thérapeutique et démarche du pardon," *Sciences Pastorales* 13 (1994) 25-54; also his *Comment pardonner?* (Outremont: Novalis, 1992). For a practical approach, see Judy Logue, *Forgiving the People You Love to Hate* (Ligouri, MO: Ligouri Publications, 1997).

The issue of forgiveness takes on a new intensity when wrongdoing that had been largely anonymous assumes a concrete, human face. In South Africa, as the killers of prominent figures such as Steve Biko and Chris Hani came to be known, forgiveness seemed nearly impossible to imagine. What does the Christian message of forgiveness mean in any of that?

A useful place to begin is by distinguishing between divine and human forgiveness. Christian forgiveness takes some of its distinctive features from modeling human forgiveness upon divine forgiveness. Yet there remain differences between the two.

The Jewish and Christian scriptures make it clear that it is God who forgives sins (cf. Lk 5:21). Jesus scandalized those at table with him when he forgave the sins of the woman who had washed his feet (Lk 7:49): "Who is this who even forgives sins?" In John's account of the upper room, Jesus bestows on the disciples the power to forgive sins through the power of the Holy Spirit; it is not something they have of themselves.

God is the forgiver of sin, not simply because God has infinite power, but because God is also the horizon of infinite love. Divine forgiveness has to be seen from the vantage point of God's love. God's love is such that any sin can be overcome. That great love began when God created the universe and the creatures within it. It was that love that was evident in the Incarnation and in the suffering and death of Jesus. That love is the power of the resurrection and of the great reconciliation toward which the entirety of creation is moving. God's constant proffering of love is at once the offer of forgiveness and the opportunity to renew a broken union or to deepen that union. When humans accept God's love, they are able to experience this greater union and also come to see the extent of their wrongdoing. They are able to come to repentance. To see forgiveness within the horizon of love does not trivialize the nature of sin. The suffering and death of Jesus show how costly divine love is. Divine forgiveness, then, has to be seen from the vantage point of this freely and constantly offered love, this desire for deeper communion.

Human forgiveness, that is, human beings forgiving one another, starts from a different point. It is about not being controlled by the past. It is the possibility of having a future different from the one that appears to be dictated by past wrongdoing. Forgiveness is an act of freedom.

Human forgiveness involves both a process and a decision. The process is one of coming free from the power of the past. To become free of the power that wrongdoing can work upon us involves the telling and retelling of the story of the traumatic event, as was discussed in the previous chapter. One cannot simply will to be free of a traumatic past; one must go through the difficult task of acknowledging the wounds and working through the memory that keeps the wounds present to us. For nearly everyone, coming free of the past is usually a long and difficult task. If the past event is the loss of a loved one, even when that loss had been expected, it takes at least a year to come free of the event. In cases of social trauma, it takes years, sometimes decades. Even then, truly coming free of the past may be possible only for a younger generation that did not directly experience that traumatic past.

Even if the process of coming free from the power of the past is achieved, it still takes a conscious decision to forgive. Arriving at the decision to forgive is, first of all, an indication that freedom from the past has been attained: it shows that one is no longer bound to the power of that past. Second, the assertion of personhood entailed by deciding to forgive is symptomatic of a certain healing of a damaged humanity. The victim no longer reacts only passively to events, but is able to steer a course through them and even beyond them. Third, a decision to forgive is a commitment to work to achieve a different kind of future. Not only is the victim no longer controlled by the past; the victim also takes steps to develop a very different kind of relation to it.

Human forgiveness, then, is deciding for a different future. It does not mean ignoring or forgetting the past. To ignore or forget the past is to demean the victim, to trivialize the suffering that the victim has undergone. Such demeaning activity can hardly be called a restoration of humanity. (We turn to the idea of "forgiving and forgetting" shortly.) Nor is it a condoning of what has been done. That would be an even more direct attack on the victim's humanity.

It is important to reflect for a moment on the traumatic deed and the effects of the deed. Sometimes a past deed can be partially undone. If something was stolen, it can be returned. There can be some form of restitution. Punishment does not undo the deed. It may fill a need for revenge, an act of counter-violence against the wrongdoer. It may also serve as a deterrent so that the wrongdoer (or others) do not repeat the deed. But the deed still stands. This is especially the case when the victims are dead. They cannot be brought back by any act of restitution or punishment. And no one can forgive on behalf of the dead—that relationship is frozen in the moment of its perpetration. Survivors may forgive, in the sense that they decide to come free of the effect that another's killing has on *them*, but they cannot forgive on another's behalf.

From this it begins to become clear that forgiveness is really not about the deed that has caused the trauma. It is about the relationship the victim has to the deed's ongoing effects. While the deed may be partially undone, it cannot be erased. No one can give full health back to a victim of torture. One can at best ameliorate some of its worst effects upon the victim's health. That a victim can forgive is a sign that the victim has arrived at a place where one is freed of the deed's capacity to dominate and direct one's life. By that is not meant that the trauma no longer has any effect on the victim. The disappearance or death of a loved one, the experience of torture, and other human rights violations create effects that cannot be erased. Forgiveness means that the balance of power has passed from the traumatic event to the victim. The victim chooses the direction of the future, and does not follow the trajectory laid out by the traumatic event. One goes from being a victim to being a survivor. A survivor does not live autonomously or indifferently regarding the trauma. That, in many instances, is impossible. Surviving means, quite literally, that there is life after the experience of the trauma. The decision to forgive is the ritual act that proclaims the freedom of the survivor to have a different future.

Before continuing to explore human forgiveness, something must be said of so-called honor-and-shame cultures. There are cultures where "honor" or "saving face" requires never forgiving. To forgive in such settings is considered to be a sign of weakness or betrayal of solidarity with one's family or group. The decision never to forgive in such a culture reveals a special configuration of power. To say "I can never forgive him for that" is an assertion of the power of the aggrieved party to reverse the relation and make the wrongdoer into a victim. The wrongdoer becomes beholden to my refusal to forgive the deed. The wrongdoer is held in my thrall. When seen in this way, to forgive the wrongdoer would bring disgrace upon the aggrieved party; it would be an admission that the victim is unable to dominate the wrongdoer.

Jesus' preaching of God's forgiveness was an attack on this kind of honor-and-shame culture.[3] True power is not in holding others in thrall. True power is in forgiving. God manifests divine power precisely in proffering forgiveness. So Jesus urged the practice of forgiving upon his followers. Forgiving is the sign of the greatest of powers—the power of God. Moreover, if there were no forgiveness, there would be no change in relations. Nothing new or better could ever happen. Precisely because the reign of God is about transformation, it is necessary to forgive. Jesus, as the final prophet of that divine reign, mediated God's forgiveness and forgave, and then passed that power to forgive on to his disciples.

Forgiving in honor-and-shame cultures may be considered a sign of weakness, but the forgiveness that Jesus preached was forgiveness growing out of love. And genuine love carries with it vulnerability. The difference between vulnerability and weakness is that vulnerability is something freely offered, whereas weakness is an unwanted deficit of power. Vulnerability is a manifestation of the trust that is at the basis of self-giving in love.

Honor-and-shame cultures cannot be so facilely deconstructed as this discussion of forgiveness within them might suggest.[4] The fundamental issue that the challenge of forgiveness raises within them, however, helps clarify an important point: *the power to forgive is different from the power to do harm.* The power to

---

[3]For a discussion of Jesus' culture as one of honor-and-shame, see Bruce J. Malina, *The New Testament World: Insights from Cultural Anthropology* (Atlanta: John Knox Press, 1981), 25-50.

[4]For a discussion of the complexity of the dynamics of these cultures, see Stella Ting-Toomey (ed.), *The Challenge of Face-Work: Cross-Cultural and Interpersonal Issues* (Albany: State University of New York Press, 1994).

forgive comes ultimately from God. It is the power of the cross, a power arising out of the vulnerability of love. The power to do harm comes from the power to coerce and to control. That is why trying to force someone to forgive—as happens all too often in Christian circles—is such a contradiction in terms.

For the Christian, divine and human forgiveness intersect at the point of the decision to forgive. The ability to decide to forgive comes from the restoration of humanity that is the grace of reconciliation. That restoration comes from the God who loves and who forgives. It is not that God is forgiving the victim; that would be to misread the situation here. God's love is what both restores the victim and, in making of the victim a new creation, also makes forgiveness possible. Forgiveness is an acknowledgement that the victim is now a new creation, and in a position to imagine a different future.

All this having been said, forgiveness is not made any easier. How does one enter into forgiveness without simply pronouncing the words in a meaningless fashion? If we acknowledge the pain that wrongdoing has caused, and the ongoing damage its effects continue to create, we must find concrete ways to enter the process and engage God's forgiveness within our own. One such way is suggested in the writings of St. Luke. Luke's gospel and the Acts of the Apostles present Jesus and Stephen, respectively, calling out for the forgiveness of their executioners: "Father, forgive them; for they do not know what they are doing." "Lord, do not hold this sin against them" (Lk 23:34; Acts 7:60). Notable in both accounts is that neither Jesus nor Stephen themselves forgive their executioners. Jesus, as we have seen, pronounced the forgiveness of sins on a number of occasions. Even in the same scene on Calvary, he appears to forgive the sins of one of the criminals being executed with him (Lk 23:43). And this occurs in the text after Jesus has called upon God to forgive his executioners. So both Jesus and Stephen call on God to forgive their executioners, but they do not utter words of forgiveness of their executioners themselves.

Is this an ironic or bitter act on the part of Jesus and Stephen, in the manner of saying "I hope that God forgives you, because I surely do not"? I do not think so. Both Jesus and Stephen in these stories see the enormity of the wrong that is being done to them. In their current state, as it were, they cannot fully grasp its import or its extent. But they feel united still to God, and call upon God to forgive. God is the source of all forgiveness; ultimately only God can forgive sin. And only God has an ample enough perspective to encompass the enormity of the evil that is now being perpetrated.

Part of the strategy of execution—certainly in the case of crucifixion—was to debase the condemned person as much as possible. The person so condemned to die was presented as a piece of human trash. Stripped and hanged for public display and derision, the humiliation did not end even in death. The bodies were unceremoniously dumped in the garbage after execution. Everything possible was done to say that this person was less than human. That Jesus could call out to God to forgive his executioners means that, although he had been stripped of his dignity, he had not been stripped of his humanity. He was still in communion with his Father. It was then up to God to forgive. Stephen's attitude toward his executioners was intended to show Stephen as the ideal disciple of Jesus, following the way of his master.

This poses an important model for those who have been subjected to terrible wrongdoing, and are then urged to forgive the wrongdoers immediately. The admonitions of bystanders to forgive may be well intentioned, based as they are on Jesus' mandate to forgive and to love one's enemies. But they do not take into account the very human dynamics of pain and suffering.

Encompassing the pain of evil done can take many, many years. In the midst of that, our own frailty in knowing how to respond becomes all too evident. To call on God to forgive is a first step toward the ability to forgive the wrongdoer oneself. By calling upon God, the victim acknowledges that forgiveness comes from God and implicitly asks to participate in God's forgiving activity, that is, to be able to see the situation of the wrongdoer in some measure as God sees the situation. It is the beginning of a process by which the victim hopes to be able to come to forgiveness. Most victims must go through a process of coming to know the consequences of the evil done and to see how evil has changed their lives. While they are making these painful explorations, they are at the same time invited to trust in the mercy of God, who is the source of all forgiveness. This more realistic way of looking at forgiveness preserves both the dignity of the victim and the capacity of God to forgive.

That is what is behind Jesus' injunction to forgive seventy times seven times and to love our enemies (cf. Mt 18:22). Jesus has unique insight into the mercy of God. When one sees things from God's perspective, as it were, then evil can be comprehended and forgiveness can occur. As we experience God's gracious restoration of our own humanity we can come to appreciate how God restores the humanity of the wrongdoer. Our own experience of being forgiven our sins should bring us to a deeper appreciation of how God works forgiveness in the lives of others. All of us have done things of which we are ashamed, things that we know were sinful. Our own experience of being forgiven can help us, even as victims of others' wrongdoing, to comprehend how wrongdoers might be forgiven.

Dietrich Bonhoeffer, the German theologian who was executed for his resistance to the Nazis, was very concerned about the confession of sin and the forgiveness of sins. As he put it once, "Only those who are in a state of truthfulness through the confession of their sin to Jesus are not ashamed to tell the truth wherever it must be told."[5] Our own confession of our sins reminds us of the mercy of God, and helps prepare us to live a praxis of forgiveness.[6]

Forgiveness in the Reconciliation Process

Where does forgiveness come in the reconciliation process? The common-sense answer is this: first comes repentance on

[5]Dietrich Bonhoeffer, *The Cost of Discipleship* (New York: Macmillan, 1963), 155.

[6]Developing a praxis of forgiveness in our families and in our communities can involve meditation on stories of forgiveness, and other exercises. Geiko Müller-Fahrenholz, a German theologian who worked in Costa Rica for many years, has brought together both meditations and exercises for communities in his *Vergebung macht frei. Vorschläge für eine Theologie der Versöhnung* (Frankfurt: Otto Lembeck, 1996).

the part of the wrongdoer, then the victim forgives, and then there is reconciliation. There must be some act of apology or acknowledgement or repentance by the wrongdoer. Guilt must be admitted. Then the victim can summon up forgiveness. And then wrongdoer and victim can be reconciled. It all seems clear enough. For this reason, after a time of strife and conflict, people will call for the wrongdoers to repent and be punished as a way of starting the reconciliation process. Unfortunately, that rarely happens in the social arena. The wrongdoers are often still too powerful to be coerced to submit to such a process. Or an amnesty is extended that protects the wrongdoers from being legally accused of wrongdoing and punished.[7] People then despair of any genuine reconciliation taking place.[8]

Social reconciliation, especially on a national basis, has to follow in some fashion this common-sense process of *repentance* → *forgiveness* → *reconciliation*. The process will have to be marked by key ritual moments that symbolize the movement through the various stages. This seems necessary because of the macrodynamics of societies. More will be said about this in Part II, when social and personal reconciliation are discussed.

At a more face-to-face level, however, a different process seems to prevail. Here the process begins with the victim, who experiences God's healing power. This power leads the victim to call upon God to forgive the wrongdoer, and then moves the victim him- or herself to forgive the wrongdoer. The wrongdoer's experience of being forgiven by the victim leads the wrongdoer to repentance. Instead of *repentance* → *forgiveness* → *reconciliation*, we have *reconciliation* → *forgiveness* → *repentance*.

---

[7]See for example Ludger Weckel, "Menschenrechtsverbrechen und Versöhnung. Zum Gebrauch des Versöhnungsbegriffs in Kirche und Theologie," *Zeitschrift für Missionswissenschaft und Religionswissenschaft* 79 (1995): 305-312.

[8]Space does not permit a detailed analysis of this. Daan Bronkhorst, in *Truth and Reconciliation: Obstacles and Opportunities for Human Rights* (Amsterdam: Amnesty International, 1995), draws upon the wisdom and experience of many people in responding to this dilemma. One who figures prominently is José Zalaquett of Chile. For the role of the churches, see the very helpful collection edited by Canadian theologians Gregory Baum and Harold Wells, *The Reconciliation of Peoples: Challenge to the Churches* (Maryknoll, NY: Orbis Books, 1997).

At first sight, this does not seem to be right. But if we recall what has been said here about the Christian understanding of reconciliation, this way of proceeding begins to make sense. Reconciliation is the work of God. God goes about restoring the damaged humanity of the victim. The victim, with humanity now restored, is once again the subject of his or her own history, and not simply an object which is acted upon by the wrongdoer. The victim calls upon God to forgive, and God out of infinite mercy does so. The experience can lead to the repentance of the wrongdoer, who may for the first time, with the help of God's grace, be able to begin to comprehend the kind of evil he has done.

This pattern seems to go in the opposite direction of the pattern of social reconciliation, and the two types of reconciliation—personal and social—may seem to be at odds with each other. That is not necessarily the case, for two reasons. First of all, as we shall see in Part II, personal and social reconciliation do not have entirely the same goals. Personal reconciliation is about the restoration and healing of a damaged humanity; social reconciliation is about the reconstruction of a more just and safe society in which the violence of past wrongdoing will be prevented from occurring again in the future. The quest for social reconciliation is a process that is intended to help bring this new society about. That there will be different processes is indicative of the slightly different (but not contradictory) goals of the two types of reconciliation. Second, it should be noted that no social program of reconciliation will be successful unless it has in its leadership a cadre of reconciled individuals, or at least people who understand the difference between the two types of reconciliation. These are the ones who have the eyes to see what can and must be done, and are able to imagine a future not ruled by the past. Think what the South African situation might have looked like if a normal politician, and not a Nelson Mandela who had been shorn of hatred in his long imprisonment on Robben Island, had tried to lead the transition from apartheid to democracy. Mandela is an example of a reconciled person. In my own work in the last five years I have been privileged to meet many such reconciled persons whose lives can only be described as crafted by the hand of God.

It is an urgent task of those who work for reconciliation to create spaces and craft communities where reconciled individuals can emerge. As we build the body of Christ, as we create genuine peacemakers for our communities and our societies, the goal of our ministry of reconciliation is to create space for and to accompany reconciled persons.

Forgiving and Forgetting

"Forgive and forget," we have often been told. It seems to be the Christian thing to do. Many Christians believe that "forgive and forget" comes from the Bible, since it sounds like something Jesus would have said.

Actually it is nowhere to be found in the Bible. As far as anyone has been able to trace it, the saying seems to go back to the Middle Ages, perhaps the fourteenth century. Why is it so frequently invoked?

There is a certain wisdom to the idea. If we kept all our past enmities alive, society would be even more conflicted than it now is. It would be impossible to maintain the network of human relationships. We all know families in which certain people will not speak to each other because of some past hurt that they are not able to forgive. Yet if nothing were ever forgotten, the whole world would be strangely silent! Forgiveness makes social change possible.

On the other hand, to urge the forgetting of painful memories and events is to either trivialize the events themselves (saying, in effect, that they were not as serious as you remember), or to trivialize the victim (you are not significant enough to have been offended that much). To urge victims to forget is to victimize them once again, saying that they could not possibly be as hurt as they claim to be.

The whole question of remembering past pain and forgiving the wrongdoer might better be phrased in this way: *In forgiving, we do not forget; we remember in a different way.* We cannot forget what has happened to us. To erase part of our memory is to erase part of our very identity as persons. But we can remember in a different way after we have experienced reconciliation and extended forgiveness. We remember now in a way that does not carry rancor or resentment for what has been done. We remember now from God's perspective, as it were, thanks to the grace of reconciliation. God does not forget what has been done to those who have been created in the image and likeness of God (Gen 1:26). But the memory can now be constructive. Take the case of the couple who lost their only child. At first they remembered the loss of him in a way that gave full vent to their feelings of anger, remorse, and refusal to be consoled. But after the experience of reconciliation, although they still mourned him and missed him very much, they remembered his goodness and kindness to others and sought to make that central in their memory. This kind of remembering builds up a human life, rather than choking it in a smoldering anger that cannot be quenched. Pain should not be forgotten, and often cannot be forgotten. We will explore this point more in the following chapter when Jesus confronts his own wounds.

We do not forget; we remember in a different way. The "forgetting" that we do in forgiving is an overcoming of anger and resentment, a being freed from the entanglements of those emotions and their capacity to keep us bound to an event. The freeing act of forgiving, done in its own good time, releases us from that bondage. In that sense of forgetting, then, we do forgive and forget—we forget inasmuch as we are no longer bound by those same negative emotions to the past.

Part of the experience of the resurrection for the disciples, then, was the experience of forgiveness. They experienced Jesus' forgiveness even before they could ask for it. This is the sign of the power of reconciliation within Jesus. And they received the power to offer God's forgiveness to others. Roman Catholics often think of this power to forgive as given to the Eleven in view of their leadership of the community of Jesus. It might be better to see it as given, in the first instance, to the whole Church as a gift. Within the Church that gift is exercised in a number of ways, and in a special way in the sacrament of reconciliation.[9] But when forgiveness of sins is seen as some-

---

[9] See Kenan Osborne, *Reconciliation and Justification: The Sacrament of Penance and Its Theology* (New York: Paulist Press, 1990), 24.

thing given to the whole Church, then it becomes a calling to be a community of forgiveness, where people can come and experience the forgiveness of God, where those struggling to forgive can find strength. Dietrich Bonhoeffer was concerned precisely with forming such a community of forgiveness at the seminary of the Confessing Church in Finkenwalde. A community of forgiveness begins with a confessing of sin. In confessing sin one comes to learn to speak the truth. And establishing the truth against the skein of lies that wrongdoing weaves is foundational for reconciliation.[10]

Food

Although the texts of Luke and John about the disciples gathered together do not say explicitly where the disciples had assembled, there has been a long tradition that the place the disciples chose to gather on that first day of the week was the upper room where they had shared their last meal with Jesus. Jesus, who had so often shared a table with them, who had used meals as opportunities to teach, was best remembered in such a setting. In Luke's account, food is certainly present; Jesus asks for something to eat and is given a piece of broiled fish. When one thinks about it, it is interesting how often food comes up in the appearance stories. We shall see it again in chapter 6 in the meditation on John 21:1-17.

On a superficial level, the food can be seen as evidence that Christ was physically present, that he was able to take in food. But there are two more rich ways of looking at this preoccupation with food. Eating together had been a principal hallmark of Jesus' ministry. He frequently referred to eating together as a sign of the peace of God's reign, where all would sit down together and the poor would have enough to eat. To eat with the disciples now showed not only that he had forgiven their lack of faith, but that the reign he had promised was now

---

[10]For a discussion of Bonhoeffer's theology and practice of forgiveness, see Jones, op. cit., 3-33.

coming into being. Second, Jesus chose to be remembered by eating and drinking together: that tradition of giving thanks, breaking bread, and sharing the cup we call the Eucharist. It is the central symbol by which we remember Jesus in the sacramental traditions of Christianity.

The Eucharist is celebrated as a foretaste of a reconciled creation, where sins have been forgiven and all feel included. Peace, forgiveness, and food come together.

CHAPTER 5

Healing Wounds

(John 20:24-29)

Thomas the Doubter

The story of Jesus' encounter with Thomas is another favorite Easter appearance story for many. Thomas is absent when Jesus appears for the first time to the disciples and, upon hearing the news that Jesus has returned, will not believe it. Only if he can see Jesus and touch his wounds will he believe. The next time that Jesus appears to the disciples Thomas is present. Jesus presents himself to Thomas and invites him to touch his wounds. Thomas's doubts drop away and he falls down to worship Jesus, saying, "My Lord and my God."

People are sometimes too hard on Thomas when they tell this story. After all, after Jesus' ignominious death it would not have been easy to believe that Jesus truly had been raised from the dead. His death had so devastated the hopes of his disciples that believing in him and his message barely seemed possible any more. To believe in what seemed impossible—that he was back from the dead—was to be almost naive.

Thomas is brought to faith in a reconciling act on Jesus' part. He does not upbraid Thomas for his lack of faith, something he surely had a right to do. Instead, he invites Thomas to touch his wounds, to see for himself that this is truly Jesus standing before him. Not only is Thomas's faith confirmed; he is overwhelmed by the tenderness and graciousness of Jesus.

We witness here the moment when the grace of reconciliation floods Thomas's heart. He is more than just cured of his unbelief; he is transformed in his confession of faith. The grace that has touched Thomas's heart is now extended by Jesus to all who have not seen yet believe: "Blessed are those who have not seen and yet have come to believe" (Jn 20:29).

It is good to pause again to recall the manner of Jesus' appearances. To Mary Magdalene, to the disciples on the road to Emmaus, to the disciples in the upper room, and now to Thomas: Jesus appears as he needs to be seen. His mode of appearance is fitted in each instance to the particular anguish in the hearts and minds of those to whom he appears. Mary Magdalene is disconsolate at the disappearance of Jesus' body. The tomb is no longer a place to mourn but has become a place of bitter absence. Jesus displaces that absence with a very physical sense of presence. The two disciples on the road to Emmaus had lost hope, and were fleeing Jerusalem. Jesus sets their hearts burning and they go running back to the holy city to tell the Eleven and their companions. Jesus himself appears, and brings peace and forgiveness to the troubled and guilty disciples in the upper room. And now he restores faith to Thomas.

In appearing in each of these distinctive ways, Jesus offers us a role model of the one who works for the reconciliation of others. The grace of reconciliation has so transformed the reconciler that the reconciler no longer has to approach the other from the reconciler's own perspective. The reconciler is now free to approach those needing healing from the perspective that will best help them. In our own ministries of reconciliation, it is important to bear this in mind. By walking with those who have been hurt, we need to come to know their stories so well that we become freed from our own perspective, and are able to enter into their worlds as fully as possible. Put another way, our being reconciled enables us to be ministers of compassion, which means literally, "to suffer with." Our compassion is deepened through the experience of our own sufferings. As we become companions of those who suffer, we develop a certain kinship in suffering. In uniting our own suffering to Christ's, we become configured into his suffering so that our suffering too might become redemptive. This is a theme to which we will return later in this chapter.

Transfigured Wounds

The story of Thomas makes much of the nail marks in Jesus' hands and the wound in his side. Biblical scholars have often said that this emphasis on the wounds in the story was aimed against those Christians who believed that Christ was not a real human being, but was an angel or a spirit who only pretended to be human. The evangelist is countering that belief by emphasizing the reality of Jesus' body, saying that this is the same body that had hung on the cross and had endured the torment of the soldiers. Luke's account of Jesus' appearance to the disciples in the upper room, when he shows them his wounds, has a similar purpose, to assure the disciples that this is indeed Jesus of Nazareth.

Scholars who say this are probably correct. But there is another aspect of Jesus' wounds that is even more intriguing in the story. Why are the wounds still visible on the transfigured body of Jesus? In these same stories Jesus is able to appear and disappear. He comes into a room even though the door is securely locked. In the Lucan account, at first the disciples do not even recognize Jesus. So his resurrected body is not just the resuscitated version of his earthly body; it is something utterly transformed.

If this is so, why does he still bear the scars of his torture and execution? If one were transforming the body of someone who had died such a terrible death, would the wounds not be the first thing that someone would want to eradicate? Would one not wish to erase the signs of that terrible experience? Why are the wounds still there?

Perhaps they are there as a kind of identification, so that the disciples can know that the one they are now seeing is truly Jesus. Luke seems to make this point in his account: "Look at my hands and my feet; see that it is I myself" (Lk 24:39). The wounds are there to assure the disciples that this really is the Jesus of Nazareth they have known and walked with along the roads of Galilee. But if that is the case, they do not serve this purpose very well. In all of these accounts, the disciples do not at first recognize Jesus. Mary Magdalene mistakes him for the caretaker. The disciples on the road to Emmaus think he is a traveling stranger. The disciples in the upper room are afraid that he is a ghost come to haunt them. If the wounds were meant to be a form of identification, they only helped identify Jesus after he had been recognized.

I would like to suggest a different reason. The wounds are not there primarily to create a contrast between what Jesus has gone through in his torture and death and what he has now become in his resurrected glory. That meaning is certainly there, but it is not the primary one. I believe the wounds are still in evidence because they are part of the message of the resurrection, of why Jesus appears at all: they are healing wounds, instruments of reconciliation.

Wounds as Instruments of Reconciliation

What does this mean: healing wounds, instruments of reconciliation? To understand, we need to think again about the role of memory in reconciliation. In the previous chapter, it was said that when we forgive, we never forget, but we remember in a different way. Memory is central to our identity as a people and as individuals. If we try to describe ourselves to others, we usually will talk about certain things and events in our past that were very important to us. We will talk about our marriage, the birth of our children, and important events that had a significant effect upon us. We will talk of the places where we have worked and of the people whom we encountered there. We will speak of people whom we have loved, and who have loved us. We will talk of the tragedies that have struck our lives and how they have affected us. What we choose to remember, and how we remember it, is central to the making of our identity. That is why the loss of memory, either through cerebral accident or the onset of illness or age, can be so frightening. Not to be able to remember means we no longer know who we are.

Memory is something we construct and constantly change, as experiences are added and others are forgotten. As we grow older, we have clearer memories of things in the distant past, but may have trouble remembering what happened yesterday. As our memory is reshaped, so too is our identity.

But what about memories of trauma? Are there not things that are too terrible to remember, that we would just as soon forget? Memories of terrible accidents, of war, of events that filled us with fear? Often even if we would want to forget these things, they are so seared into our memory that we cannot forget them. Sometimes they so overwhelm our memory that they are constantly before us. They wake us up in the middle of the night and we tremble with fear. We cannot go in certain places or see certain things without those terrible memories coming right back to us. I remember one woman telling me that she could no longer go down a street in her neighborhood because her son had been killed there in a traffic accident. The sight of that street made all those memories rush back for her. Like a tape playing over and over again, those painful memories come back to us.

Among the most traumatic memories are those experienced by survivors of torture and other forms of physical abuse. In these cases the trauma is literally inscribed on their bodies. It is not just something they saw or heard, it is something they have felt etched into their very flesh. The body has an extraordinary capacity to hold within it memories and the emotions associated with them. In what is now called post-traumatic stress disorder (PTSD), physicians trace how memories can literally take over the body.[1] Not only in mended bones or scarred-over wounds, but deep in the tissues of our flesh those memories perdure.

Torture is especially evil because its very purpose is to rob the victim of autonomy and trust. The torturer tries through the systematic infliction of pain to inscribe the message that he has complete power over the victim. The victim can try to resist, but that will not bring an end to the torment. The victim can scream, but no one can hear and no one will come to the victim's aid. The victim has all shreds of dignity and autonomy stripped away. And the victim is meant to feel deeply alone. No

---

[1] Perhaps the most accessible book on PTSD is Judith L. Herman, *Trauma and Recovery* (New York: Basic Books, 1982).

one—not even God—will rescue the victim. It is that profound aloneness that works to destroy the humanity of the victim. When one is so utterly alone there is no one to trust. Solitary confinement in prisons tries to produce that aloneness. Prisoners create imaginary dialogues in their minds to combat this aloneness by recalling and maintaining past connections and relationships. They remember lists of things and conjugations of verbs, and they play mental games, because lists and games mean connections. Relations and connections are what keep us human.

Traumatic experiences, especially those inscribed on the body, play themselves over and over again in our minds like a never-ending tape. They can eventually block out everything else and literally take over our lives. In cases when the physical pain of those traumas persists, it constantly reminds us of what has happened. Sometimes it is the flash of memory into our consciousness that brings back the fear and the suffering.

Most people who have been through such experiences need help overcoming them. If they cannot be overcome, they may pull us down into the abyss of absence, that black hole of nothingness. We need someone to help us. The help that is given is one of accompaniment and listening. The story must be told over and over again until the pain starts to lessen. Sometimes it must be acted out physically to relieve the memory of the body. Those who accompany and listen have to create a space of safety where trust can be relearned and a damaged autonomy can be examined and gradually rebuilt. If the victim has been confined, even the simplest of daily routines must be relearned. The persons who accompany and listen are the ones upon whom trust is built as victims begin to recover what has been taken away from them.

Do people ever recover from these experiences? Many do not. They cannot stop the tape of their memory playing over and over again in their minds, and it gradually breaks them down. It is like a weight that gets heavier and heavier which makes life ever harder to bear. Some are driven mad by it. A few even end up taking their own lives.

Others achieve a measure of healing. They become survivors. This means that, although they can never be completely rid of these terrible experiences, they are able to reconstruct their lives in considerable measure. The traumatic experience will remain a defining element of their lives, but it will no longer have the same devastating effects. Those who have achieved this most successfully are able to help others through the long ordeal of having their humanity restored.

The experience of reconciliation is coming to that turning point when survival becomes possible. That which was taken away is now restored, but not so as to bring victims back to where they were before the trauma—the continuing relation to the trauma forecloses that possibility—but to a new place where a more or less normal life can be taken up again. One way of existing in the new place is to develop a mission that involves relating with the trauma in a creative way. Often survivors help other victims become survivors. They find in the restoration of their own humanity the vocation to help others with theirs. There have even been a number of stories of survivors meeting their torturers and, because they had been restored to their own humanity, they were able to be concerned about the humanity that their torturers had lost.

Jesus and His Wounds

The risen Jesus is a survivor. He has been through abuse and torture. He has been beaten, mocked, and had thorns pressed into his head. He has experienced public humiliation and been executed on the cross. He has experienced the pit of death. And now he has been raised from the dead.

We cannot get inside Jesus' own experience of this. Piero della Francesca's painting of Jesus risen tries to capture what might have been part of that experience. Jesus looks a little dazed or bewildered, as though this will take some getting used to. The experience of resurrection life has nothing with which it can be compared. It is not the same as resuscitation from death, as Lazarus experienced, for those who have been so resuscitated die once again. In the appearance stories, Jesus' body is indeed glorified, but the scars of his torture remain. His body has both discontinuity and continuity with his past.

It is interesting to see how Jesus deals with his wounds. In Luke's account of the appearance in the upper room, Jesus volunteers to show the disciples his wounds. It is as though he is a little amazed about them himself. These are wounds that do not go away, but link Jesus forever to his passion and death. In this, Jesus is like every survivor who must bear the burden of those wounds for the rest of his or her life. Jesus shows the disciples his wounds and talks about them freely, because they are no longer a source of pain and painful memory, but now, in the case of Thomas, become wounds that heal. They heal Thomas's troubled soul, riddled with the loss of faith and hope. Jesus' wounds have a remarkable quality, therefore. They link him back to his own death, but point ahead to life and hope as well.

But how do wounds heal? How do they make someone else whole? Wounds, first of all, mark a break in the surface of things. A smooth surface does not prompt reflection or thought. It takes the disruption of that smooth surface to give us pause to ponder. Wounds are an invitation to become aware of how fragile the human body is, how easily it is penetrated. They remind us that all our arrangements, personal and social, can be easily disrupted. The violence that wounds do to the tissues of a body—cutting through the delicate layers, disrupting the functions—puts into question how much we can rely upon things to be as they should be. Wounds are question marks about existence.

An open wound allows us to peer inside the body, below the surface of things, and to discover there that what is underneath is not like what first appears to the eye. We see structures and processes that support the surface but look very different in themselves. We become aware that so much of our world is not what it seems. To reach this realization may undermine trust for some. That wounds can occur, that they can be deliberately inflicted, makes the world a very unsafe place. For others, it is an invitation to contemplate the complexity of the world and how much human flourishing relies on a capacity to trust. Trust itself is as fragile as those broken surfaces we contemplate, yet without trust there is no full human life.

In the previous chapter, we touched on the relation of vulnerability to the process of forgiveness. Vulnerability—literally, the ability to be wounded—is a kind of self-giving in love that makes possible coming to a new place, a new state of existence. Vulnerability is not about masochism, or a desire to draw attention to oneself or to be pitied. Vulnerability is a capacity so to trust that one runs the risk of wounds. It does not make wounds desirable, nor does it make them less painful. One is willing to run the risk of wounds because of something more important: the communion of love that engenders trust, that makes the fresh start of forgiveness possible.

When Thomas is invited to touch Jesus' wounds, those wounds draw out of him the disruptions below the surface of his own life. His trust has been shaken, his faith in Jesus as the messenger of God's reign has been called into question. Touching the wounds of Jesus connects his inner wounds to those very visible ones of Jesus. The wounds of Thomas's heart can be placed in the larger and deeper wounds of Jesus' hands and side. In this way, Thomas is healed and can move from doubt to his confession of faith.

Wounds have knowledge. Those who have suffered physical wounds that have changed their bodies know how a change in weather can signal itself in their old wounds. Onsets of tension or stress sometimes register in the same way. And wounds may also be the point where the decline of age announces itself. When those wounds are touched, or when environmental changes make them ache, the memories of their infliction instantly come back. Wounds bear, therefore, a kind of knowledge. They become repositories of memories of traumas that are now past, but whose infliction has forever altered a life.

It is the knowledge wounds bear that gives them a healing quality for others. When Thomas touched the wounds of Jesus' crucifixion, it was as though the memories in those wounds provided a way of reorganizing Thomas's own experience. His memories were no longer troubling to him, because they had been transfigured into a confession of who Jesus had become. Wounds can heal because, having the memory of trauma, they can connect to the wounds of others. They know the experience of disruption and pain. The transfigured wounds of Jesus have not lost that quality of memory. The transfiguring wounds of Jesus' crucifixion hold that memory in a special way. It is a memory that cannot be erased; it will always be part of him. But it is only such memory that can touch the trauma of memory in another.

People are usually afraid to touch wounds, either for fear of hurting the wounded person or for fear of contagion. Jesus, however, invites others to touch his wounds. His wounds have become redemptive. They heal others; they are contagious through the spread, not of disease, but of the alleviation of suffering.

The wounds of those who have experienced the trauma of war or of torture are not worn as badges of honor, although others on occasion may treat them that way. They more likely still ache than glow. But those wounds give the reconciled the possibility of entry into the wounds of others. They become healing wounds, wounds that render the wounds of others less painful. Their wounds know about healing—how long it takes, how incomplete the healing will always be. It is the knowledge of the patience needed, and the realization that wounds can always produce new pain that make the wounds of the reconciled so sensitive to the wounds of others. It is little wonder, then, that it is the reconciled who are our best leaders in any process of reconciliation.

Redemptive Suffering and Reconciliation

Healing wounds have shown us how suffering can be redemptive rather than destructive. There is nothing ennobling about suffering itself. Whether it becomes redemptive or destructive has to do with how the one suffering responds to it. In the story of Jesus and his wounds, there are two ways of seeing the redemptive character of his suffering.

On the one hand, Jesus bears the wounds of his passion and death so that we will not have to undergo a suffering that utterly destroys us. Whereas many people through the centuries have been killed by more gruesome torment and excruciating forms of torture, Christians believe that Jesus' suffering was of the most acute quality possible. This is because of who Jesus was, and the unique and complete communion he shared with his Father. Because of that communion, Jesus in his death destroyed the ultimate power of death to separate us forever from God. Liturgically, this truth is captured in the Memorial Acclamation of the Roman Catholic Eucharist: "Dying you destroyed our death, rising you restored our life." Jesus goes before us, bearing the pain that we will not have to bear because of what he has done. The grip that death held on us in its ability to end our communion with God has been broken. That means that all our efforts to resist in suffering are not just futile efforts flailing at the inevitable extinction of our existence. By uniting that suffering with the suffering of Jesus, by touching our wounds to his, suffering can bring us to a new place. Our suffering can become redemptive of ourselves and others.

By going before us, Jesus teaches us how to carry the pain we do have to bear, the burdens of suffering that we do have to endure. Jesus teaches us how to move from victim to survivor, how to create spaces of safety where pain can be unfolded and memories healed. He teaches us how to take the victim's perspective, how to accompany the victim as he accompanied the disciples on the road to Emmaus. He teaches us how to deal with the sense of loss that so rent the heart of Mary Magdalene. He is the silent teacher who uses his own wounds to heal the wounded hearts of others.

The other way that the wounds of Jesus' passion and death heal is by enfolding the sufferer and giving shape to the suffering. When Thomas was invited to touch the wounds in Jesus' hands and side, it was as though Jesus was taking Thomas's wounded spirit and embracing it with his own. When suffering is inchoate, it can threaten our very being. When it can be turned into redemptive suffering, that is, when it can be set in the context of a higher purpose, it can ennoble our humanity rather than debase it. It becomes the opposite of the debasing and dehumanizing pain that the torturer tries to inflict. It is the suffering of a mother in labor who endures the pain for the sake of the child that is to be born. It is suffering endured for the sake of a higher purpose. The pain of someone who is terminally ill can be transmuted into redemptive suffering when that person is able to discover the meaning of his or her life, and locate this final suffering as a moment within that life rather than merely its termination. Suffering becomes redemptive suffering, then, when it does not isolate us from those around us, but becomes a way to bind us to them in new and deeply human ways. One sometimes sees this when a terminally ill parent can work reconciliation among estranged members of the family, or when someone who is ill is able to bring a community together in a new way. The death of Joseph Cardinal Bernardin in 1996 in Chicago was such an act of reconciliation. He used his last two months of suffering to create new spaces of reconciliation within the wider Chicago community and within the Church nationally. The words of the funeral homily still ring loudly in my ears: "Didn't he teach us, didn't he show us the way?"

Christians believe that Jesus' suffering and death were not meaningless, but were redemptive of our lives. His descent into the abyss of absence restored communion between ourselves and God. The cruelty he experienced restores our humanity. He not only taught us how to suffer, but he takes up our pain in his own suffering so that it can be life-producing rather than death-dealing for us. Our suffering is not the end of us, but a moment on the road to full communion with God.

Christ shed his blood so that our suffering, rather than being destructive of us, would become a pathway to a transformed self. Christ's blood stands as an everlasting sign that our suffering will never be in vain. That suffering may not achieve what we thought it was supposed to. Being brought to a new place in reconciliation means that our perspectives get changed, and we can see things that we had not seen before. It may be that we shall never quite see, but are asked instead to deepen our trust and confidence in Christ so that we might become more fully human and more conformed to him.

It is in this way that the cup of suffering is turned into the cup of hope. This change is not a setting aside of painful memories in some casual manner. It is a fermentation, if you will, that transmutes suffering to hope from the inside, slowly but unceasingly, gently but relentlessly, until our hope dawns.

A spirituality of reconciliation, then, involves finding our wounds and seeing if they can be a source of healing rather than of ever greater misery. It means placing our pain in the crucible of Christ's own suffering that our pain might find direction and purpose. As has been noted several times, reconciliation restores our humanity and brings us to a new place. It often gives us a vocation as well, a vocation that makes of our own wounds sources of healing for others. This is what is meant by a spirituality of reconciliation that reflects the glory of the resurrection.

CHAPTER 6

Breakfast on the Seashore

(John 21:1-17)

A Model for the Ministry of Reconciliation

This story about Jesus and the disciples on the shore of the Sea of Tiberias is a touching one that portrays Jesus at his most human. Here we see Jesus caring for his troubled disciples, calling to them from shore. We have many stories of Jesus eating with his disciples; this is the only one where he cooks for them. How Jesus works to heal the remorseful Simon Peter has also captured the imagination of Christians for generations.

I would like to suggest that this story recapitulates the whole ministry of reconciliation. Many of the themes that have been explored in this book come together here in a marvelous way. I would suggest we follow the narrative and examine how different themes of reconciliation come forward.

Going Fishing

This story is the only one we have of Jesus appearing in Galilee. In Mark's gospel, the angel tells the women that Jesus is going before the disciples into Galilee (16:7), but this is the only story we have where an appearance of Jesus actually takes place there. (Scholars believe that the incident of Jesus walking on the water [John 6:16-21 and parallels] may also be a resurrection appearance story retrojected into the life of Jesus.) The story starts simply enough: Simon Peter says to Thomas, Nathanael, James and John, and two other disciples that he is going fishing. They all say, quickly and eagerly, "We will go with you."

This all sounds innocent enough. They are, after all, fishermen. But if we start to look beneath the surface of this seemingly simple event, other things begin to appear. We must remember that the disciples have returned to Galilee from Jerusalem. It was in Jerusalem that they had hoped that Jesus would usher in the reign of God of which he had spoken. Instead, they were confronted with the terrible shock of his arrest, torture, and execution. They had left Jerusalem—either out of fear for their own lives (since they had been followers of someone executed as an enemy of the state), or out of disappointment (something like the disciples on the road to Emmaus). After arriving in Galilee, they try to get back to a normal life. Simon Peter announces that he is going back to what he did before: fishing. The Jesus story is over. It is time to pick up the strands of the life he had had before meeting Jesus. It is time to forget the whole Jesus story and try to live a normal life again. The disciples with Simon Peter are only too eager to join in. Going back to fishing will take their minds off what has happened to them.

But it does not work. They are out on the water all night and cannot catch a single fish. Try as they may to get back to a normal life, things just do not work out right. They feel frustration as they try harder and harder but still come up with nothing.

People who have been through a great trauma such as the end of a dictatorship or release from prison can recognize what Simon Peter and the disciples are feeling. They want to distance themselves as quickly as possible from the pain they have endured and the horrors they have seen. They try to pick up their shattered lives and lose themselves in the ordinary ways of doing things. They want to be able to forget what has happened to them and be led along by the familiar routines of day-to-day living. Or, as has happened in some countries after they have been liberated from authoritarian governments, they try to lose themselves in consumerism and desire. It is as though they hope that consumerism and pleasure will blot out all the unpleasant memories of what went on in those fateful years.

But it never seems to work. The past cannot be shut out or cordoned off so neatly and so arbitrarily. The reverberations of pain and trauma continue to rumble through their lives, dogging them during the day and haunting them at night. Ordinary things trigger memories of a still painful past. A word, a gesture, a sound can summon up a whole scene that they have been trying to forget. The day-to-day routine does not fall into place. The glitter of consumption and the freedom to satisfy desire are not able to hold the past at bay. In those moments when their guard is down, the past returns. It is as though it still has a hold on the present even though they know it now to be past.

So it is for the disciples. They try to fish, but catch nothing. They pass the entire night, trying ever harder, but with no success. Their nets are empty. Somehow the simple pleasures of ordinary living are now denied them. Their frustration keeps reminding them of how far they have gone from that uncomplicated way of living that they remember.

Such is also the experience of many victims of violence. The quotidian experience of life seems disrupted forever. Words they hear, things they see, people they encounter can bring back immediately the trauma that they have experienced. It is as though the past is never really behind them, but is lurking alongside them, waiting to spring out in front of them at every turn.

The boat of the disciples on the Sea of Tiberias may not be laden with fish, but the disciples are carrying the heavy burdens of their past with them. Being relieved of those burdens is a long and difficult experience for most people. The disciples in the boat are like most of us, wanting to escape those burdens but finding them always still with us.

Daylight breaks. A stranger appears on the shore and asks them about their fishing. He addresses them affectionately as "children," a favored appellation of the believing community in John's gospel. The term certainly connotes the care and concern the stranger has for the disciples. This attitude sets the scene for what is to follow. When the disciples reply that they have been unable to catch any fish, Jesus suggests that they try lowering their nets on the other side of the boat. In their earnest efforts to escape the past and re-enter an ordinary life, they have been fishing, almost obsessively, in the same place. This is fairly typical behavior for those who have been victims of violence. They search obsessively in the same place for their release from trauma, but consistently are unable to find it there. The stranger's suggestion that they try fishing in another place helps them break the cycle of their obsession.

As they struggle to haul on board their nets bulging with a catch of fish, the Beloved Disciple recognizes the stranger. He echoes the words of recognition that have been heard earlier in the other appearance stories: "It is the Lord!" Suddenly they recognize who the stranger is. It is only by being freed from the obsession with finding what they had hoped would be a familiar groove of routine that they are able to recognize who has been standing on the shore. Often too for us it is only by being lifted out of the way that we are sure will lead us to salvation that we can come to recognize the salvation that is being presented to us.

Simon Peter, upon hearing that it is the Lord, throws some clothes on, jumps out of the boat, and goes splashing through the water to reach the shore. We might well wonder what was going through his mind. After the frustrations of not catching any fish, through the seemingly miraculous draught of fishes, and then the realization that it was Jesus who was standing on the shore, a great number of things must have been coming to mind for Peter. The sudden plunge into the water reveals Peter to be as impulsive as ever. He seems to have learned so little from the experiences in Jerusalem. The bravado in saying that he would never betray Jesus, the impulse that had caused him to draw his sword in the garden at the time of Jesus' arrest, and now the leap into the water and the rush to the shore: this is very much the same old Simon Peter.

What will he say when he gets to the shore? There stands Jesus, the master whom he has denied even knowing. Those clothes quickly donned will not hide his shame nor mask his remorse for what he has done. What does he expect from Jesus? A word of reproach? Did Peter hear in Jesus' calling them affectionately "children" the hope for release from his burden of betrayal?

Hospitality on the Shore

The disciples are no doubt surprised to find that not only is Jesus standing there on the shore, but there is also a charcoal fire, on which some fish are cooking, and also some bread. Jesus invites them to add some of the fish that they have caught to those fish already cooking. And then he says, "Come and have breakfast." This is certainly a surprising way to encounter the risen Lord! The narrator recounts that the disciples are left speechless by this invitation from Jesus.

We have already seen how Jesus appeared to the disciples in the context of eating a meal, since this was a way that they would have remembered Jesus. This story goes a step further. Jesus not only shares a meal with them, but he prepares it himself! To the notion of the shared fellowship of a meal Jesus adds the important concept of hospitality. He is the one to prepare a meal for the disciples. He acknowledges what they have brought along (their newly caught fish), and then serves them breakfast. He, their Lord, is also their servant. The breakfast has its own irony. Jesus is cooking fish for these fishermen who have not been able to catch any fish, and who had given up his commission to be "fishers for people" (Mt 4:19; Mk 1:17). With the fish is bread, which has come to be the sign of his absence and his presence. Bread and fish together recall the story of the multiplication of the loaves and the fishes (Mt 15:32-39; Mk 8:1-10), a sign of God's abundance. They portend the abundance of the grace of reconciliation that is about to flow into the disciples' hearts. A new day is indeed breaking.

In showing hospitality, Jesus once again sets the scene for reconciliation. He created an atmosphere of listening to hear the stories of the saddened disciples on the road to Emmaus. In the upper room in Jerusalem, he created a safe environment for the disciples to come to terms with their fears and accept forgiveness. And now, on the shore of the Sea of Tiberias, as the sun is rising, he makes the disciples breakfast.

What we have seen Jesus do thus far can be called the first two steps in a ministry of reconciliation. First, Jesus watches intently as the disciples fail to catch any fish. He senses that catching fish is not the issue here. Jesus had called them away from being fishermen to become fishers for people, that is, to gather the people into the reign of God. But the disciples had wanted to go back to catching fish. Jesus gently moves them out of their obsession with erasing the recent past by surprising them with a huge catch of fish where they had not expected to find them. The ministry of reconciliation begins with a careful but intense accompanying of victims. This accompaniment is marked by a listening patience that allows the victim to reveal that which is a burden, even when the victim cannot be articulate about what that burden is and why it weighs so heavily. Most of us do not have the instant insight that Jesus seems to have in urging fishing in another place. But we must remember that this is not Jesus' first encounter with this group of would-be fishermen. He has known them for a long time, and he calls upon that memory to aid him in meeting them again.

Accompanying victims calls for that same patience and care that Jesus shows the disciples. Victims of violence have had bonds of trust cut to shreds. Their world has been so altered that they do not know whom or what to trust. Their old routines offer no comfort. Jesus' calmness helps the disciples negotiate the difficult reality in which they find themselves.

Then comes the hospitality, the second moment in the ministry of reconciliation. Jesus knows how to create a hospitable environment. He cooks familiar food for the disciples, and then he serves it to them. He knows to ask for some of their fish, so that they can feel that they have contributed to the meal. For people who have lost all routine, he restores one of the routines that mean the most: sharing food together. A hospitable environment exudes trust and kindness. It also creates an atmosphere of safety. For victims of violence, trust, kindness, and safety are the things most sorely lacking in their lives. An atmosphere of trust makes human communication possible again. Kindness reaffirms that violence is now past and provides a space for the vulnerability required by healing. Safety is the other side of trust. For those who have lived through threats and danger, the restoration of safety allows the bonds of trust to be rebuilt.

Hospitality carries with it also a sense of gratuity, a graciousness that is not measured in a quid pro quo manner, but in an abundance that invites thinking about new possibilities.

One of the difficult aspects of reconciliation is coming to terms with the violence that has been done to the victim. In assessing the damage that has been done—be it the loss of loved ones, the destruction of one's home, torture, or imprisonment—we try to imagine for ourselves what it will take to redress the wrong. That is what many people mean by the word "justice." But reconciliation does not take us back to redress the wrong along a path that we chart out for ourselves. Reconciliation always comes by a different route. As was seen in chapter 4, we do not forget the past but learn to remember it in a different way. That ability to remember in a different way does not grow out of a calculating calibration of the wrong and its redress, but from the abundance of life we call grace. That is why hospitality, which sets up an environment of trust, kindness, and safety, is the prelude to reconciliation. It helps prepare victims for the welling up of God's healing grace in their lives, for the restoration of their humanity. It is a restoration, not in the sense of returning them to a previous, unviolated state, but in the sense of bringing them to a new place.

Hospitality, then, is central to the ministry of reconciliation. So much of the ministry of reconciliation is about waiting and listening: waiting on God, learning to be transformed by the discipline that waiting entails, and developing a listening heart. Hospitality, on the other hand, is something that we can do. Here we can take the initiative to create an environment in which reconciliation can happen.

It is important to recall that hospitality must occur in forms that the victim understands. Patterns of hospitality are specific to each culture, and knowing the nuances of what counts for hospitality in any given culture is essential to the exercise of hospitality in that culture. In this story, Jesus gives the disciples food that they recognize: fishermen eat fish for breakfast! He prepares for them not only fish that he has caught, but fish that they have brought along, *their* fish. It has been noted several times that Jesus appeared to the disciples as they needed to see him. This reconfiguration of the self or the community in the act of hospitality is important if the hospitality is to be effective. Most of us have been in situations where we have received hospitality to which we did not know how to respond. We know how uncomfortable and self-conscious we feel in such situations. A genuine hospitality takes into consideration the guest and the guest's expectations. We see Jesus doing that in this story.

Reconnecting and Commissioning

After breakfast is over, Jesus turns to Simon Peter. Note that Jesus does not begin his questioning during breakfast. Hospitality has its own place and its own priority. Part of the experience of its gratuity, then, is that it is not used for any extraneous purposes: it is there for its own sake. But when breakfast has been completed, Jesus is ready to move into the next stage.

"Simon, son of John, do you love me?" These simple words must have struck Simon Peter forcefully. After all, he had denied knowing Jesus and had utterly abandoned him. But Jesus does not ask him whether he knows who Jesus is. Jesus does not ask for recognition, nor does he bring up the painful memory of Peter's being huddled around another charcoal fire outside the high priest's house in Jerusalem (Jn 18:18). Rather, Jesus asks: "Do you love me?" He addresses him only as "Simon," rather than as Simon Peter, the name he had given him as a leader among the Twelve. The issue here is not Simon Peter's leadership, but Simon as a person who carries the wound of having betrayed Jesus.

Simon Peter, impulsive as ever, hurriedly answers, "Yes, Lord; you know that I love you." The answer may have come from impulse, but it is nonetheless genuine. Yes, he does love Jesus. And, more important, Jesus knows that Peter loves him despite what Peter has done. Jesus knows Peter in all his weakness and impulsiveness.

Jesus' reply to Peter comes as a surprise. "Feed my lambs," Jesus says. Jesus does not say that he forgives Peter for what he has done, although that is clear in his reply. Here Jesus is moving on to the third and fourth steps in a ministry of reconciliation. By asking Peter whether he loves Jesus, rather than whether he recognizes Jesus (which would have undone denying that he knew him), Jesus reconnects Peter to himself and to the community.

Reconnecting is the third step in a ministry of reconciliation. Victims are often disconnected or even isolated from the
community. That is what acts of violence set out to do. They
say, first of all, that victims have lost their dignity as human beings, that they deserve to be excluded from the human community. Refugees, cut off from their homes and families, experience this. The most extreme example of the experience of
exclusion is torture, where the victim is systematically and de-
liberated isolated, and this isolation and violation are inscribed
on the victim's body.

Reconnecting is about ending the isolation that severs trust
and presses victims to believe the lies the wrongdoer tells about
them—that they are not worthy of human treatment, that no
one can rescue them, that they are despicable. Violence strives
to inculcate that lie, that hatred of self, in victims, knowing that
self-hatred will keep them in the bondage of victimhood. Reconnecting is the reaffirmation of truth about the victim, that
the victim is made in the image and likeness of God and therefore of inestimable value.

That is why Jesus speaks of love rather than any adjudication of the wrong that has been done to him. Jesus has forgiven
Peter. The grace of the resurrection was the grace of Jesus' humanity being restored to him after his ignominious torture and
death. Indeed, reconciliation is an experience of resurrection,
of partaking in what God has done for us in Christ.

The fourth step in the ministry of reconciliation is commissioning. Jesus does this for Simon Peter by telling him to feed
his (Jesus') lambs. Jesus has not only reconnected him to the
community of Jesus and his disciples, he has given him a specific charge and task within that community. He is once again
Peter, the rock upon which the community is built. Out of the
experience of reconciliation, we have seen, a vocation often
also emerges. Here Simon Peter is called to his vocation, of caring for Jesus' flock. The vocation to which the reconciled person is called often has a dual connection. There is a connection back to the experience of violence. Such is the case, for
example, when reconciled survivors of violence work with
other victims of violence. It is part of remembering in a different way. The other connection looks forward, often to work so

that the conditions that permitted the violence to occur do not happen again. We see this dual connection in the commissioning of Peter. He who once denied knowing Jesus is now charged with keeping Jesus' memory alive in the community of disciples. He whose denial betrayed trust is now entrusted with the little flock of Jesus' lambs. His vocation, his commission, allows Peter to remember his own past in a different way, and to help create a community where trust is nurtured so that denial will never happen again.

Jesus asks Peter three times if Peter loves him. Three times he commissions Peter to care for the community of Jesus' disciples. Peter is anguished by being asked three times. Does Jesus not hear his sincerity? Is this Jesus' way of punishing him for his denial, by making him go over it again and again?

What Peter does not understand in this threefold asking on Jesus' part is the power of ritual in healing and reconciliation. Jesus' three queries constitute a ritual way of undoing Peter's three denials of Jesus.

Ritual is an important aspect of reconciliation in a number of ways. First of all, ritual's repetitive nature underscores how difficult it can be to come to terms with the past. Peter's denial of Jesus had cut deeply into Jesus' heart. By asking not once but three times, Jesus subtly underlines the depth of pain the denials caused and why multiple forgiveness is necessary. The repetition in ritual intensifies its effects. In this instance, that intensification underscores the gravity of the denial that is being undone.

Second, the continuing need for the victim of violence to tell his or her story over and over again is evidence of how ritual repetition can untangle the skein of lies to bring forth truth. Victims tell their stories over and over until the stories begin to change and to open up new perspectives. It is often in this way that the grace of reconciliation comes to them. They can never completely stop telling their stories, even after they have experienced reconciliation; to do so would erase the past. But they come to be told in a different way. The ritual retelling of stories, especially at key times (anniversaries, commemorative moments), is a way of reinforcing identity and reaffirming the change that has taken place. The Last Supper narrative that is retold in every celebration of the Eucharist functions precisely in this way: by recalling that story we are bonded to Christ anew.

Third, ritual action overcomes time. It allows us to experience past events in the present, and to anticipate what is hoped will happen in the future. To remember Jesus in the ritual action of the Eucharist connects us back to his time and connects us forward to the eternal banquet in heaven. That ability to transcend time is important for reconciliation because it allows us to escape the tyranny of traumatic past events. We can find ways of relating to them that respect the integrity of memory but liberate us from the painful bondage.

Fourth, the formal nature of ritual helps us give public, common shape to experience. We do not understand entirely how ritual works, but its formal character creates a space in which a difficult and conflictual past can be dealt with, and a certain closure can be brought to the experience. Since the past cannot be undone, ritual actions in the present can blunt its power and transform it from something death-dealing and victimizing to something transforming and life-giving. In the story of the South African woman who wanted the new government to buy a tombstone for her murdered son, the tombstone would not bring him back to life, nor would it compensate the woman in her loss. But it would stand as a symbol of acknowledgement of what the apartheid government had done, and as a reminder to future generations that such terrible acts must never be repeated. Ritual, in this way, can mark coming to terms with the past so that it can be remembered in a different way.

This ritualized moment made the difference for one woman and her family. Margaret J. Smith recounts how the decision to bring home the remains of a soldier who died in World War I and re-entomb them in the Hall of Memory of the Australian War Memorial in 1993 in Canberra effected national healing and reconciliation. Australians had been used by the British as cannon fodder in many battles in World War I, most notoriously at Gallipoli. This powerful ritual event brought healing and closure to those terrible memories.[1]

---

[1]Margaret J. Smith, "The Order of Christian Funerals: Process of Remembering and Hoping" (D.Min. Thesis, Catholic Theological Union, 1994), 21-25.

Jesus closes this act of reconciliation by predicting the kind of death that Simon Peter will die. When that moment comes, Simon Peter will not deny Jesus. Restored to his humanity by the risen Jesus, he will witness to his belief in his Lord.

The Ministry of Reconciliation

At the beginning of this chapter, I proposed that this story of Jesus at the seashore was a model of the ministry of reconciliation. Let me summarize the four steps in that ministry and add some concluding comments. The four steps are accompaniment, hospitality, making connections, and commissioning. As ministers of reconciliation, we are most proactive in the first two steps. Learning how to accompany, and learning how to create through hospitality an environment of trust, kindness, and safety are disciplines that can be studied, practiced, and learned. To be sure, some people by inclination and temperament will be more suited to this than others. The impulsive Simon Peter, after all, was probably not very good at accompaniment; he was always rushing ahead, as he did when he jumped out of the boat into the water. But we can learn how to do it, and we can create communities that sustain these ministries of reconciliation.

Communities of reconciliation have three important aspects. First of all, they are communities of safety, zones in which victims can examine and explore their wounds. The experience of violence is the opposite of the experience of safety. The memory of the violation of human rights has to be replaced by an assurance that such things will not happen again. Safety is the basis for the rebuilding of trust. The practice of nonviolence in communities of safety is an important sign to victims that here they will not be sucked back into the vortex of violence.

Communities of reconciliation are, second, communities of memory. They are places where memory can be recovered, a memory that is redemptive of the suffering of the past and not a continuing destroyer of persons and communities. Even more important, a community of memory is a place where a people can come to common memory of the past, for "a society cannot reconcile itself on the grounds of a divided memory."[2] For a past truly to be overcome, people must come to a common memory of it. Otherwise the divisions of the past are perpetuated in the present. Communities of memory are also places where we learn again to speak the truth. If people have lived under authoritarian governments for a long time, even though they try to resist its effects, they can find themselves distorting the truth and drawn into the lies their overlords imposed upon them. Worst is the self-loathing that results from lies inscribed on the bodies of the victims of torture. One of the aims of torture is to get the victim to believe that he or she really deserves the torture.

Third, communities of reconciliation are communities of hope.[3] They are places which nurture the seedlings of a better, more just world in the future. They bring people beyond a culture of endurance, which has allowed them to survive on a day-by-day basis, to a culture of hope which can envision a future in the longer term. As with communities of memory, communities of hope work to build a common future in which all are safe, justice is done, and the truth is told.

Returning now to the steps in the ministry of reconciliation, the third and fourth are making connections and commissioning. Whereas the first two steps—accompaniment and hospitality—can be achieved through human endeavor, these last two are both very much the work of God. The connections made are often surprising and unexpected. They are ultimately made by the victim, since the making of those connections is part of the experience of being restored to full humanity, of being the subject of one's own history. Think back to the Emmaus story. The disciples had the words of the Jesus story right, but they were struggling to make the connections. When the connections that change the story are finally made, the mo-

---

[2]Alex Boraine, Janet Levy, and Ronell Scheffer (eds.), *Dealing with the Past: Truth and Reconciliation in South Africa* (Capetown: IDASA, 1994), 13.

[3]The phrases "communities of memory" and "communities of hope" come from Josiah Royce. See his *The Problem of Christianity* (Chicago: The University of Chicago Press, 1968; originally published in 1913), 248.

ment of insight is often experienced as a divine intervention in the victim's life.

Similarly, the commission, especially when it has a dual connection to the past violence and to a future without violence, is often experienced as being given by God rather than chosen and constructed by oneself. Like the connections, commissions too also have an element of the surprising or unexpected.

As ministers of reconciliation we can only mediate in indirect ways those connections and commissions; we do not create them. The spirituality needed for a ministry of reconciliation is best developed in that learning to wait and listen that marks good accompaniment. We may end up helping the restored victim identify connections and commissions, but we are not their source.

Finally, what should be apparent by now is that reconciliation is the fruit of the resurrection. To read the appearance stories as stories of reconciliation helps to understand both what resurrection and what reconciliation are about. Exploring how we, as people of the resurrection, are also ministers of reconciliation will be the subject of the next chapter.

CHAPTER 7

"Taken from Their Sight"

(Acts 1:6-11)

The End of the Appearances

The appearances of Jesus after the resurrection did not go on indefinitely. The scriptures tell us that forty days after the resurrection, Jesus appeared to the apostles for a final time. On that occasion, as they were all together, he commissioned them to be witnesses to the resurrection "in Jerusalem, in all Judea and Samaria, and to the ends of the earth." The text goes on to say, "When he had said this, as they were watching, he was lifted up, and a cloud took him out of their sight." As they were still gazing up, they were addressed by two men in white robes: "Men of Galilee, why do you stand looking up toward heaven?" (Acts 1:8-11). Their task at this point was not to gaze after Jesus, but to go forth to be witnesses to the resurrection.

The remarkable period following the resurrection had come to an end. The disciples had gone from being frightened into silence at the sight of the tomb, to having their hearts burn as Jesus opened the scriptures for them, to receiving forgiveness and the power to forgive, and now to a commission to be witnesses of what they had seen and heard "to the ends of the earth." The meaning of the resurrection had gone from being a concept without clear meaning to an experience of forgiveness, healing, peace, and reconciliation. The disciples had gone from disappointment and confusion to a boldness in proclaiming the message of what God had done in Jesus.

Now they entered a new phase, one in which they would no longer see the risen Lord, but experience his Holy Spirit in the gathered community, in the breaking of bread and the sharing of the cup. The message of the resurrection would continue to be proclaimed. It would be in the Eucharist, that sharing of the bread and cup, that Christians would experience at once the presence and the absence of the Lord—his presence in the intensity of the bonds that the community shared, in the prophetic word that would be preached; and his absence in that yearning for the Lord to come again "in the same way as you saw him go into heaven" (Acts 1:11).

Resurrection and Reconciliation

We now turn again to our own time, here at the end of a violent century, and ask: what is the message of the resurrection for us today? And what does it mean for us as people who work for reconciliation? What does it mean to be a resurrection people?

In this concluding chapter of Part I, I would like to step back from our close reading of the appearance stories and explore the meaning of the resurrection, now that the Lord has been taken from our sight. What is being proposed here is that, following Philippians 3:10, we must be conformed to Christ's death in order to know the power of his resurrection. To look at the resurrection as endless Alleluias is to hollow out its profound meaning. To rejoice without recounting what has brought us to this place is to make empty sounds. The resurrection appearances were not merely opportunities to prove that Jesus had been raised up from death or to manifest his divinity. They hold within them Jesus' own efforts to work reconciliation in the lives of his disheartened disciples who had been traumatized by his death. From the power of his resurrection, he gave himself to be seen as each of the disciples needed to see him: Mary Magdalene, Simon Peter, Cleopas and his companion on the road to Emmaus. In those encounters they came to experience what God had done in raising up Jesus and how it had healed their lives from the devastation that they had experienced. They learned to remember the death of Jesus in a different way: not merely as a brutal torture and ignominious death as an enemy of the state, but as a cosmic act that reconciled the world to God through the mediation of that death, "making peace through the blood of his cross" (Col 1:20).

The resurrection of Jesus is rich in meaning, and through the centuries it has been read in many different ways. It has been seen as a triumph of the forces of light over the powers of evil and darkness. It has been hailed as a liberation from captivity. Here I have stressed seeing it as dynamic reconciliation. Understanding the resurrection as reconciliation helps us realize the profound connection between suffering and reconciliation. The suffering of victims is not simply annulled and forgotten in the reconciliation process. To obliterate suffering in that manner demeans the victim and the victim's experience. The suffering is not forgotten, but the memory of it is transformed and remembered in a different way so that, its story taken up in the story of the Lord's own suffering and death, it can be made into something life-giving for others. The victims will always bear the wounds of their suffering, as does Jesus. But those wounds now can heal and give life to others even as they bear testimony to what the victim has undergone.

The resurrection is about truth. In his speeches in the Acts of the Apostles, Peter makes the point over and over again that the message which evildoers wanted to convey in executing Jesus had been nullified by God. Jesus' being raised from the dead spoke the truth about Jesus and what God thought of him. Reconciliation, as I have tried to show, is about truth. The violence perpetrated against victims is fundamentally a lie about their existence and how they stand before God. That is why truth is essential to justice. Justice without the pursuit of truth can turn into revenge. The truth is what ultimately undoes the lies of the evildoer and the evildoer's abuse of power. Pope John Paul II has captured the relation of truth to justice, especially as it relates to forgiveness, in his message for the 1997 Day of World Peace. He says that there are two things required to bring about forgiveness and reconciliation: respect for the truth and a justice "that is not limited to that which is right among the parties in conflict, but looks above all to reestablish authentic relations with God, with the self, with others."[1] Truth prepares the ground for justice.

A spirituality of the resurrection, then, is a spirituality of reconciliation. Through Christ's resurrection, the most heinous of tragedies that have befallen men and women can be healed. The resurrection can do that because of what Christ himself suffered and because of his own descent into death.

A Resurrection People

What does it mean to be a resurrection people, committed to a ministry of reconciliation? The third chapter of the letter to the Colossians is a meditation on that very question. Let us hear once again some of the verses from that remarkable text:

> But now you must get rid of all such things—anger, wrath, malice, slander, and abusive language from your mouth. Do not lie to one another, seeing that you have stripped off the old self with its practices and have clothed yourselves with the new self, which is being renewed in knowledge according to the image of its creator.... As God's chosen ones, holy and beloved, clothe yourselves with compassion, kindness, humility, meekness, and patience. Bear with one another and, if anyone has a complaint against another, forgive each other; just as the Lord has forgiven you, so you also must forgive. Above all, clothe yourselves with love, which binds everything together in perfect harmony. And let the peace of Christ rule in your hearts, to which indeed you were called in the one body. And be thankful. Let the word of Christ dwell in you richly....
> (Col 3:8-10, 12-16)

These words are worth meditating upon, since they provide a blueprint of what a community of reconcilers—themselves rec-

---

[1] John Paul II, "Offri il perdono, recevi la pace" (Messagio per la celebrazione della Giornata Mondiale della Pace - 1 gennaio 1997), *L'Osservatore Romano* (18 diciembre 1996), p. 5.

onciled—would look like. Notice the stress on truth, and the avoidance of lies: "do not lie to one another." The virtues of compassion, kindness, and patience were discussed in the previous two chapters as aspects of the ministry of reconciliation. Compassion is the quality of accompaniment. Kindness is a mark of hospitality. And patience is needed in all things. The exercising of the ministry of forgiveness, discussed above, marks the community of reconciliation. And love binds everything together. The word of Christ must come to dwell in us richly. It is the word of the suffering, death, and resurrection of Jesus, that great story into which we can place our little stories so that the suffering does not destroy us, but brings us to that transformation in grace that is reconciliation.

Can we really become communities of reconciliation? In nearly every country in the world today there are wounds of division that call for healing and reconciliation. Even if a country has had truth and reconciliation hearings, the wounds still remain. Even if some of the wrongdoers have been punished, healing has not been completed.

Today the conflicts that are springing up in the wake of the end of the Cold War are producing numerous situations where reconciliation and healing will be needed. Relief agencies— even secular relief agencies—are turning to the churches to ask them how to bring the resources of their traditions of reconciliation to bear on societies that have been torn asunder by war and violence. The hundred million refugees in the world cry out for a healing of their hearts. Those who have been silenced by war and oppressive governments are seeking to find their voice, a voice that must be heard. The victims trampled under the headlong rush of neo-liberal capitalism must be redeemed. To echo the psalmist: "Truth shall spring out of the earth, and justice shall look down from heaven" (Ps 85:12 [NAB]).

A spirituality of reconciliation based on the resurrection is surely a spirituality for these times. In the resurrection of Jesus we see the risen Lord at work in healing divisions and bringing about a new life. The call to us to be ministers of reconciliation (2 Cor 5:18-19), bringing near in the blood of Christ what was once far off, breaking down the wall of hostility that separates us (Eph 2:13-14), is a call to reconciliation rooted in truth and struggling for justice. It seeks the truth that will not be suppressed, that continues to spring out of the earth among the poor, the dispossessed, and the downtrodden. It awaits the justice that comes down from heaven, that is, a justice that goes beyond retribution to create a human society as God intended it.

This understanding of reconciliation, of the peace made through the blood of Christ's cross, illumines what the resurrection can mean for our time. It is not a forgetting of the past, but a transfiguration of it. It seeks peace, it engages in practices of forgiveness. Surely we could not ask for a more challenging and timely spirituality than this! It is challenging because it requires us to seek reconciliation in our own families and communities. It is challenging because it requires us to sustain communities of reconciliation that can provide accompaniment and hospitality to those seeking reconciliation in their own lives. And it is timely, especially as we see the sad directions our world seems to be taking.

The message of the resurrection is that hope is possible, a hope that is rooted in the peace of Christ, gained for us in the great reconciliation which God is effecting. That reconciliation is being brought about in all the smaller acts of reconciliation that take place in the world today, evidence of God being with us.

PART II

ELEMENTS OF A STRATEGY
FOR RECONCILIATION

CHAPTER 8

Two Preliminary Questions

In this part of the book, some elements of strategy for reconciliation are briefly explored. The word "elements" is chosen advisedly. As was noted in the Introduction, there are two reasons why one cannot speak of "the" strategy of reconciliation. First of all, we are still learning a lot about reconciliation itself. There are still so many efforts at reconciliation under way. Even where formal processes have been completed, it will take years to judge fully just how effective they were. Daan Bronkhorst's report on reconciliation efforts in the face of histories of human rights abuses is the best *status quaestionis* we have to date.[1] It will be some time before anything definitive and comprehensive will be able to be written.

Second, it has become increasingly apparent that no two social situations of reconciliation are alike. Reconciliation, if it is to be effective, is not an abstract idea. It is about coming to terms with a very concrete past and working toward a different future within the constraints—political, economic, social, cultural, and religious—of the context. With this in mind, it is good to begin any reflection on a strategy for reconciliation by focusing on two issues: what "reconciliation" means in this context, and who the actors are in the reconciliation process.[2]

---

[1]Daan Bronkhorst, *Truth and Reconciliation: Obstacles and Opportunities for Human Rights* (Amsterdam: Amnesty International, 1995).

[2]For an exemplary exploration of these two questions in the context of South Africa, see Mark Hay, O.M.I., "Ukubuyisana: Reconciliation in South Africa" (D.Min. Thesis, Catholic Theological Union, 1997), 158-184.

Defining reconciliation in a given context is an important part of the initial stage of the reconciliation process itself. It involves coming to some measure of agreement on (1) what and who need reconciliation, (2) what will be the efficacious means for bringing that about, and (3) what the final state of reconciliation will look like. The purpose of pressing these three questions is to create as much as possible a common discourse among all involved. Because reconciliation is never broached as a subject unless there is deep division within a society, one should not expect that anything close to unanimity (or even consensus) will ever be reached. Pressing these questions, however, is important for bringing to the surface the agendas of the parties involved. An example of what happens when this is not done may be found in the second ecumenical assembly of the European Council of Churches, held in Graz in June 1997. Because there was no prior agreement on the issues of what needed reconciliation or how reconciliation should proceed, the assembly broke down as a cohesive working unit. Different groups each lobbied for their own agenda.[3]

As to the first question, who or what needs reconciliation, there must be some consensus about what needs reconciling. Wrongdoers and victims will have different perspectives on the answer to that question. Wrongdoers are likely to say that there is nothing that needs reconciling. What was done in the time of violence had to be done. Victims will point to very specific acts that need to be addressed. Those who consider themselves as not having been directly involved are likely to want to get the whole thing over as quickly as possible, and so will opt for some token, hasty act of reconciliation.

There can be different levels in the analysis of the problem as well. Attempts may be made to try to seek reconciliation for the resolution of the most obvious wrongdoing (say, human rights abuses), or they may address deeper causes that laid groundwork for the wrongdoing (say, land ownership). In es-

---

[3]For one account of the failure of the meeting see the reports in *Le monde* (1e juillet 1997): "Le malaise des Eglises orthodoxes a assombri le rassemblement oecuménique de Graz," and "Gays, Verts et féministes dans la nouvelle Babel," 6.

tablishing a reconciliation process in Rwanda, for example, is the issue needing reconciling the terrible slaughter that took place after the death of President Habyarimana, or should one go back to the inequities established between Hutus and Tutsis under Belgian colonial rule? Can there be agreement on where to begin?

One must also ask: Is a reconciliation process the best way to deal with the issue, or are there other means of adjudication (for example, the legal system)? Continuing the line of questioning: What will happen to the society if some form of reconciliation does not take place?

The second question, about the efficacious means of bringing about reconciliation, raises a further question regarding just what the appropriate means are. Cultural issues need to be taken into account. Thus, reconciliation patterns already available in Mende culture helped move along the reconciliation process in its early stages in Sierra Leone.[4] To import another kind of reconciliation process may not be effective; such a process might prove to be unintelligible in a given setting. For example, in one of the Rwandan refugee camps, children were given crayons so they could draw their feelings of trauma. Instead of drawing, the children ate the crayons. They had never seen crayons before, and they were hungry.

Other constraints may intrude on the process. If the legal system has been totally discredited by its identification with the previous regime (or has literally been wiped out, as was the case in Rwanda), what can take its place? In Rwanda, new lawyers and judges were hastily trained, and a tribunal was convened in Tanzania to start dealing with all the human rights abuses. Time may also be a factor: How many resources can be committed to a reconciliation process, and for how long? New governments frequently want the past to be dealt with quickly so that national energies can be focused on reconstructing the society. (The call for speedy disposition of the past often also comes from those who were complicit in the wrongdoing.) A further constraint on the means for reconciliation may be the

---

[4] Communication from Brian Starken, C.S.Sp. This was the case, at least, prior to the coup in April, 1997.

fact that the powers that were responsible for the wrongdoing are still very much in power. Such was the case in Chile after democratic elections were held: General Pinochet, who had been dictator since 1973, was still head of the Armed Forces, and would issue veiled threats if efforts at dealing with the past were not to his liking. In the case of civil war that ends in a mediated settlement, there are likely to have been human rights abuses on both sides, so that there are no "neutral" parties that might make up an impartial board for hearings. One solution to this has been to grant both sides amnesty.[5]

Finally, there must be an ongoing discussion about what the final state will look like. To be sure, reconciliation does bring the parties to a new place, and that new place cannot entirely be anticipated. This, however, is not a reason to forgo a process of imagining what the reconciled state will look like. While the discussion may not itself produce the outlines of the reconciled state (or at least one that all sides can agree upon), it is important for the community of discourse to be established. As we shall see in the discussion of social reconciliation in the next chapter, the process of seeking reconciliation is an important part of reconciliation itself.

Naming the actors in the reconciliation process is a matter of identifying the groups who need to be considered in the reconciliation process and their relation to that process. Mark Hay has identified eight such actors in the reconciliation process.[6]

The first are the *victims* and the *survivors*. Recall from chapter 5 that victims become survivors when they experience reconciliation and the past no longer controls their lives. Survivors take a leading role in the reconciliation process. For both victims and survivors, the reconciliation process is of central importance. It must speak the truth about the past and bring to light what the authorities tried to hide. It must result in at least some measure of justice for the victims. It must also build some kind of guarantee that such terrible things will not be visited upon the victims again.

---

[5]Such was the case in El Salvador. I am grateful to Aronet Díaz de Zamora for insight into this.

[6]Hay, op. cit., 175-183.

The second are the *wrongdoers* who have perpetrated the crimes. Their interest in the reconciliation process is to get it over as quickly as possible and with least damage to themselves. They will be keenly interested in issues of amnesty and pardon. They will try to subvert anything in the process that might put them in an unfavorable light or cause them to be punished. To the extent that they maintain power in the new arrangement, they will try to block there being a reconciliation effort at all.

The third are the *bystanders* who, while not having been directly involved in or directly suffering the consequences of the violence, nonetheless are at least tacitly complicit because they looked the other way when the abuses were carried out. Bystanders share the wrongdoers' wish that the process be over as quickly as possible. They harbor the fear that somehow they might end up being implicated. A guilt for not having done more will well up inside them.

The fourth are those who were both *victims* and *wrongdoers.* Such groups have perhaps the most difficult agenda in a reconciliation process, because they must go through what both victims and wrongdoers go through. They will find the roles at conflict within them. Such conflicted people emerge frequently in the aftermath of civil wars, where human rights abuses have occurred on both sides. In other cases, members of the oppressed group were co-opted or coerced to work on the side of the oppressor. During Guatemala's civil war, for example, many of the ordinary soldiers in the army sent to suppress the indigenous people in the countryside were themselves indigenous. East Germans who spied on their neighbors for the Stasi are yet another example. In all these instances, members of this group have to sort out both being victim and being wrongdoer.

The fifth are the *dead.* Even though they are not participants in the reconciliation process, they exercise a powerful presence in its proceedings. Finding out what happened to the dead, and where their bodies now are, often takes central stage in the reconciliation process. As was said in chapter 4, no one among the living can forgive wrongdoers on behalf of the dead. What can be done, however, is to honor them properly. Such honoring (as we saw in the case of the Australian war dead) can become a key ritual moment in social reconciliation.

The sixth are the *future generations*. These are not the witnesses who lived through the violence, but those born thereafter whose lives continue to be touched by what has gone before. Think, for example, of the children of survivors of the Holocaust, growing up in countries far away from those where the atrocities occurred. How do they relate to their parents and that history? Special thought must be given in the reconciliation process to the children and how they will grow up in the time after the violence.

The seventh are the *neighbors*, either those who border the country physically or those who became involved with the struggle during the violence. Neighbors may have sided with victims or wrongdoers. Their need to participate in the process is directly proportional to the level of their involvement during the violence.

The eighth is *God*. God is a point of reference in the reconciliation process. How do the groups—and how does the process itself—stand before God? How does the process look from God's perspective, as it were?

Identifying the different actors and their agendas in the reconciliation process helps in determining where competing and cooperating moments are likely to be found. Naming the different kinds of groups can provide a kind of checklist of those to be included in the reconciliation process, and what each group needs to do to participate in and benefit from the reconciliation process.

CHAPTER 9

Individual and Social Reconciliation

It has already been noted several times that there are distinct emphases in individual and social reconciliation. It is time to present and evaluate these differences. Something will be said about each form of reconciliation, and then how the two relate to each other.

As the reader may recall, individual reconciliation occurs when the victim's damaged humanity is restored. This restoration, which may be prepared for by a supportive community offering safety, accompaniment, and hospitality, is the work of God. The experience of reconciliation brings the victim to a new place; it is not a return to the *status quo ante*. Frequently the experience of reconciliation also brings with it a commissioning or calling to undertake a special work. We saw in chapter 6, in the case of Simon Peter, that the calling can have a double connection: back to the traumatic event itself, and forward to some work relating to preventing the traumatic event and its effects from reoccurring.

It was noted in chapter 1 that social reconciliation is not the same as individual reconciliation. Nonetheless, for social reconciliation to be successful, there must be reconciled individuals present to help give leadership to the process, as well as a cadre of people who understand the meaning of individual reconciliation. Individual reconciliation helps nurture and strengthen social reconciliation, but social reconciliation cannot be reduced to individual reconciliation.

How, then, might social reconciliation be defined? Here is a definition of José Zalaquett, who chaired the Truth and Reconciliation Commission in Chile: "Forgiveness and reconciliation should thus be considered a process of reconstructing the moral order that is more healthy than punishment."[1] Here the emphasis is on the process of reconstructing the moral order of society. Each of these elements is important. Social reconciliation is a *process* that engages an entire population. All have been touched in one way or another by the violence, so all have to be engaged in the rebuilding. Social reconciliation is a process of *reconstructing* a society. It is not the building of a society where there was none before. It involves going back over the past and discovering the truth there amid the tangled lies of violence. Nor can the society be reconstructed entirely of new materials. The memories of the past perdure, and they continue to influence how the present is constructed and the future imagined. Finally, social reconciliation is a process of reconstructing the *moral order* of society. Reconciliation is a moral and spiritual work. Social reconciliation, in undertaking that work, has to use the social means available to achieve its goals. It must demonstrate a morality that will ground civil society. It uses the rule of law to institutionalize its morality. The deliberate and public use of law in the reconstruction of society is especially important when law has been used to legitimate violence and to create lies.

The three elements in Zalaquett's definition bring out the distinctive features of social reconciliation. In social reconciliation, the process of reconstruction is as important as the final product. How the process is planned, who leads it, who participates in it, where it takes place, what its stated goals are—all these elements should be planned as deliberately and carefully as possible in a strategy of reconciliation. The process should say as much about how the new order differs from the old as what actually results from the process. The symbolic dimension, therefore, is quite important. For example, if a truth and reconciliation commission is set up, who are its members? What do they represent symbolically? The place where such a commission meets is also symbolically significant. Does it meet in public or civic buildings as a way of rebuilding belief in public institutions? Does it meet in police stations or in military

---

[1] José Zalaquett in Alex Boraine, Janet Levy, and Ronell Scheffer (eds.), *Dealing with the Past: Truth and Reconciliation in South Africa* (Capetown: IDASA, 1994), 11.

barracks to counteract symbolically the abuses of human rights that took place there? Does it meet in churches, to lend a sense of sacrality to its proceedings? Where such commissions meet is not a matter of unimportance.

In many instances the process of social reconciliation *is* the final product. A society reaches a point at which it can no longer concentrate on the past and must direct its energies to the future. This leaves much undone; but at times there comes the realization that dwelling any further on the past will not lead to healing but allow in a perverse way the divisions of the past to take on new valence.

Second, social reconciliation is deeply concerned with morality. The principal moral claim in the process is justice. The many meanings of justice will be taken up in the next chapter. Important here is not justice in the abstract, but justice in the concrete cases of injustice. Justice may be a matter of addressing violations of human rights, or the restitution of what has been stolen. If the language of individual reconciliation has a strongly anthropological leaning, that is, it is concerned with the victim's humanity and capacity to relate to God, to self, and to others, the language of social reconciliation is deeply ethical, focusing on actions that need to be undertaken and deeds that need to be redressed.

Finally, social reconciliation has to be concerned that the future does not repeat the past. It must work toward guarantees that will keep the government and others from violating human rights again. Without this somehow in place, whatever new order social reconciliation provides will not be trusted.

Daan Bronkhorst lists four essential requirements for reconciliation commissions:

- They must try to get to the *truth* of what really happened during the violence. Without accounting for the dead, and trying to get at the motives of the wrongdoers, and obtaining some agreement from all sides, the country will be rebuilding itself on the basis of divided memory.
- The process must lead to a *strengthening of law*. This involves regaining respect for the law if the law was used to create and legitimate violence. It also en-

tails building into law provisions that will protect
the citizenry from such violations in the future.

- The process must be *democratic and verifiable.* As
many people as possible should participate in it, especially victims. The process should be open to the
scrutiny of both the national and the international
community.

- There should be avenues of redress and reparation
for victims, so that they can claim back at least
some measure of what they have lost.[2]

What, then, is the relation of individual and social reconciliation? The two forms of reconciliation share many characteristics. Both are about coming to terms with the past for the sake
of a better future. Both seek a state where such violations of
persons and peoples will not happen again. Both work for a
change in relations: a restoration of the humanity of the victim,
and a conversion on the part of society.[3]

There are, however, different emphases that in turn lead to
different processes. As we saw in the discussion on repentance
and forgiveness in chapter 5, the sequences of repentance, forgiveness, and reconciliation are different in the individual and
the social settings. The essential difference has to do with the
point at which reconciliation takes place in the sequence. In its
individual form, reconciliation takes place internally within the
victim and leads to the social consequence of forgiving the
wrongdoer with the hope of leading the wrongdoer to repentance. Social reconciliation is a public process that seeks repentance and forgiveness at key points along the way to a final
point called reconciliation. These different sequences have, in
turn, influence on other aspects of the reconciliation process.
For example, the reconciled person's view of what kind of justice needs to be pursued regarding a violent act in the past may
differ from that of the general public. Recall the example of

---

[2]Daan Bronkhorst, *Truth and Reconciliation: Obstacles and Opportunities for
Human Rights* (Amsterdam: Amnesty International, 1995), 150-151.

[3]On the necessity of conversion or *metanoia* for a society, see Gregory
Baum in Gregory Baum and Harold Wells (eds.), *The Reconciliation of Peoples:
Challenge to the Churches* (Maryknoll, NY: Orbis Books, 1997), 189-190.

the woman in chapter 2 who appeared before the Truth and Reconciliation Commission in South Africa to recount the abduction, torture, and murder of her son. She did not ask for punishment of the wrongdoers; she asked for the new government to provide a tombstone for her son. The woman had come to terms with the past and was focused on the present and the future. In social reconciliation, the public pursuit of justice in the process (even if what seems to constitute justice changes) is necessary for the credibility of the process and helps those participating to accept the final outcome with regard to whatever measure of justice is attained.

What this indicates is that the term "reconciliation" does not mean quite the same thing in its individual and social incarnations. Individual reconciliation, in its Christian understanding as presented here, does not appear to have great cultural variance. The reconciling moments in the Easter appearance stories speak to people of very different times and places. Social reconciliation, while having many common characteristics across cultural boundaries (as Bronkhorst points out in his study), is subject to much more cultural variance. How the different human rights are ranked, what counts for suitable justice, what will restore relationships—all of these admit of a good deal of variance from culture to culture. That does not make social reconciliation inferior to individual reconciliation as a process. It only points to its utter concreteness and rootedness in a specific history and context.

The relation between the two forms of reconciliation, however, is somewhat asymmetrical. It is possible to achieve individual reconciliation when there is no social reconciliation. The Easter appearance stories attest to that. The disciples are helped to come to terms with Jesus' violent death and its impact upon them even though Roman hegemony has been left intact. Indeed, many of them would suffer death at the hands of the same hegemony, still unchanged, years later. The Easter stories attest, however, to how reconciliation changed them as individuals and created a new kind of community.

It is hard to imagine what a social reconciliation would look like without considerable individual reconciliation. Social reconciliation processes cannot engineer reconciliation, even though they can create conditions under which reconciliation will be more likely. Even social reconciliation needs charismatic, defining moments if it is to be successful. And those moments are imagined by reconciled individuals.

To say that the relationship is asymmetrical does not make individual reconciliation superior to social reconciliation. Their tasks and their goals are similar and interconnected, but nonetheless distinct. I believe that a cadre of reconciled individuals is necessary for the success of social reconciliation. They are a necessary but not a sufficient condition for social reconciliation. Society is more than the sum of the individual members. For that reason, processes of social reconciliation are necessary to ensure the long-term survival and flourishing of reconciled persons. A society that does not attend to the requirements of social reconciliation will lapse into the nightmare from which it has awakened, perhaps into an even worse state than the beginning. Issues of truth and justice cannot be ignored.

Truly reconciled persons do not stop being concerned about the welfare of others and of the larger society when they have come to terms with their own past. On the contrary: the commissioning that arises out of their experience of reconciliation urges them into action. It is they who are the true leaders of communities of safety, memory, and hope. It is frequently they who are most sensitive to the defining moments that will help make a public difference as to how society at large will deal with the past.

Individual and social reconciliation have a measure of interdependence. Social reconciliation brings individually reconciled people to new places. This is evident in the case of people who have experienced individual reconciliation while still living under a repressive regime, but who come to a new place nonetheless when the repressive regime is brought down. This is not surprising, since no individual lives in isolation from the social environment.

What remains important is to be aware that each type of reconciliation has slightly different goals (individual reconciliation: restoration of humanity damaged by traumatic events; social reconciliation: a process of reconstructing the moral order of a society) that consequently require different processes. Both forms of reconciliation are helped by an awareness of what type of reconciliation is at stake in any given moment.

CHAPTER 10

Truth and Justice

Throughout this book the words "truth" and "justice" have appeared over and over again. No one can dispute the importance of both concepts to the reconciliation process. Both concepts carry within them a variety of meanings. This chapter looks briefly at some of the salient meanings of both truth and justice as they relate to processes of reconciliation.

There are at least three different meanings of truth that are relevant to reconciliation. Truth can mean first of all a correspondence between what happened and what is said about the event. There were instances in South Africa where the police claimed that detainees had leapt out of windows to their deaths in an effort to escape. In fact, the detainees had been defenestrated. The first account does not correspond to the facts: the detainees did not jump; they were pushed and thrown from the windows.

Truth can mean a coherence among a set of beliefs or practices. A coherence theory of truth helps explain complex events where no single act can prove or disprove a judgment. To use another example from South Africa, the accumulated human rights violations under apartheid lead to the conclusion that the regime was violent, repressive, and gravely unjust. Protestations by some white citizens that the government engaged in acts of benevolence may correspond to actual facts, but cannot negate the overwhelming record of the government's violence toward black people and those whites who stood in solidarity with them. Coherence theories of truth work by accumulation of evidence when no single item can sway the judgment one way or another.

A third type of truth is existential truth, which is a truth that is felt as illumining human experience. We often speak of the truth of an artist in this manner, meaning that the significance of an experience is caught in the work of art that has been created. Pablo Picasso's "Guernica" caught for many the truth of the Spanish Civil War. Guernica was a village bombed by fascist planes in 1938. Monuments to the dead are often set up to convey this type of existential truth.

There are other types of truth as well. Philosophers speak of performative and pragmatic forms of truth. But these three—truth as correspondence, truth as coherence, and existential truth—are singled out here because of their immediate relevance to the reconciliation process.

The question of truth arises most keenly in Truth and Reconciliation Commissions. An examination of the various ways these commissions are structured and an evaluation of their results are beyond the scope of this book.[1] What will be presented here relates to how truth is understood in the reconciliation process as a whole, and why there is a concern for truth.

Truth in reconciliation has to be understood in terms of the lies that wrongdoers perpetrate in a situation of violence, and the environment of untruthfulness that is created. Lies about individuals, about groups, about society itself legitimate the violence with which the wrongdoers control the society. Individuals become "enemies of the state," and so disappear, are tortured, and killed. Their surviving relatives and friends are stigmatized as also being suspect. Those in power legitimate their use of violence as the only means available to "protect" people from some internal or external threat. Things get turned on their heads in a version of Orwellian Newspeak.

The truth that is sought in the reconciliation process is in the first instance the retrieval of what really happened. This means cutting through the skein of lies that has been wrapped around facts and events and forcing open the doors of secrecy. Bronkhorst, drawing upon the work of Jürgen Habermas, de-

---

[1]For a comprehensive overview, see Neil J. Kritz (ed.), *Transitional Justice: How Emerging Democracies Reckon with Former Regimes* (Washington: United States Institute of Peace, 1995), 3 vols. See especially vol. 1, *General Considerations.*

fines truth as that which corresponds to the facts in a way that I can understand, from a source I can trust.[2] The truth must fit the facts as best they can be ascertained; it must be presented in a way that victims or their surviving families can understand; and it must come from a reliable source (in the case of testimony by the wrongdoers, the veracity of their reports must be confirmed by the truth commission).

Establishing the truth about what happened, especially what happened to the dead, is essential for the reconstruction of the moral order. Sometimes the truth can be relatively easy to establish, especially when the previous government kept careful records of its deeds. Nazi documentation of the deeds perpetrated in the concentration camps is an extreme example of such record keeping. Declarations of amnesty sometimes have to be given in order to elicit information from the wrongdoers.

The results of such truth-seeking must be presented in a public report. Along with the facts, the report contains immense symbolic value as a bastion against the lies that have been told. Moreover, establishing the truth is one of the few things that can be done for the dead: to know how they died, and where they are buried.

At the very minimum, this kind of truth has to be established about the events that occurred, the identities of the miscreants, and what happened to those who died. The questions about the motives that lay behind the actions of the previous government may be harder to bring to light. Motives are always complex, and the deeper the digging goes for a more abstract truth of why the wrongdoing happened at all, the more the motives blur into the evil always below the surface of a society. Nonetheless, the quest for truth should be pursued as far as it can go.

Beyond finding out what happened, truth in reconciliation processes is important for another reason. Seeking the truth establishes a pattern of truthfulness upon which a new society can be rebuilt. A public, participative search for the truth helps reestablish trust. Public practices of truthfulness go a long way in ridding a society of the mendacious and secretive practices that

---

[2]Daan Bronkhorst, *Truth and Reconciliation: Obstacles and Opportunities for Human Rights* (Amsterdam: Amnesty International, 1995), 145-146.

sustained the oppressive society. *Doing* the truth helps *speaking* the truth.

Finally, truth in reconciliation processes is especially important where very little justice is likely to be had. It has already been noted that truth may be the only justice the dead receive. General amnesties create climates of impunity that do not permit any action against known wrongdoers. Impunity is a danger to democracy, because it perpetuates the lies of the former regime.[3]

From a Christian perspective, the aim is consecration in truth (cf. Jn 17:17), a dwelling in the truth of God. It is a reminder once again of how all reconciliation is ultimately rooted in God.

From this brief account one can see how all three types of truth come into play in the reconciliation process. In accounting for the dead, truth is correspondence to the facts: what happened, when and where it happened, and where the remains of the dead now are. Likewise, for dealing with individual events, a correspondence form of truth is the most desirable.

Sometimes exact correspondence with the facts is not retrievable. Here a coherence theory begins to play a role. But, more important, a repressive government is not a series of isolated individual acts; it has to be grasped as having some kind of coherence, galvanized by a fear (of Communism in Chile, of Tutsis in Rwanda) or shaped by an ideology (Leninism in the former Soviet Union, apartheid in South Africa). Coherence theories of truth allow us to relate the diverse experiences into some form that can be understood and, in the case of repressive governments, resisted.

What reconciliation processes ultimately need, after the facts have been ascertained and the magnitude of wrongdoing has been grasped, is an existential grasp of the truth of what has happened. Here truth commission reports, and later, monuments to the dead, provide that kind of truth. For the early Christians, the Eucharist represented the existential truth of the presence and the absence of their Lord. It made the past present to them and kept their sights set on the future.

---

[3]A conference was held on this subject in Santiago de Chile in January 1997. I am grateful to Alejandro Reyes for providing me the papers from this meeting.

Existential truth emerges with the end point of social reconciliation, when one can experience the truth as something coming from God, when a people can feel consecrated in the truth.

The calls for justice are among the first heard in the reconciliation process, and rightly so. Blatant violations of human rights cannot be ignored or brushed aside. The pain that victims or their surviving families have borne must be acknowledged and addressed. A society cannot simply move from a state of oppression to a liberated state as though nothing had happened. The past, ensnarled in lies and in injustice, must be confronted.

Justice in reconciliation processes is not a univocal concept. One must examine carefully how the word is used and what meanings it conveys. Frequently the first calls for justice are for punitive justice—the apprehension, trial, conviction, and punishment of wrongdoers. The blood of Abel cries out from the earth (Gen 4:10). Care must be taken that the justice sought is genuinely punitive justice and not simply revenge. The desire for vengeance is understandable in light of the heinous things that have been done, especially in cultures where revenge is sanctioned. The rage, the anguish, and the helpless feeling converge to make a powerful denunciation. But countering violence with more of the same will not aid in the reconstruction of a society. It will simply stoke the embers that will flare up in a future conflict. Croatian-born theologian Miroslav Volf captures the suspicion about the calls for truth and justice that may indeed be something else when he says that "there is far too much dishonesty in the single-minded search for truth, too much injustice in the uncompromising struggle for justice."[4]

The call for punitive justice has to be channeled into the reconciliation process. The sad thing is that sometimes little can be done about bringing the wrongdoers to justice. This only heightens the frustration on the part of victims or their surviving families, leading to allegations that nothing can be done in the reconciliation process until punitive justice has been exercised. But there are at least three other levels of justice that come into play in reconciliation.

---

[4]Miroslav Volf, *Exclusion and Embrace: A Theological Exploration of Identity, Otherness, and Reconciliation* (Nashville: Abingdon, 1996), 29.

One is a restitutional justice, which seeks to make amends by providing reparation or restitution for victims. This may mean, as it did in Chile, funds to provide for the education of children whose fathers disappeared. It may support those widowed in the human rights violations, or provide health care for those whose health was irreparably damaged by torture or other ill-treatment. Restitutional justice is a symbolic act that admits that a full and complete justice cannot be done: the dead cannot be brought back, or health may never be fully restored. It represents, however, an act on the part of the new government to make amends in some measure for the harm that has been inflicted. It also presents the picture of a government caring for its citizens rather than seeking to do them harm.

A second level might be called structural justice. It is aimed at the structural inequities of a society that were the source of the conflict that led to the violence. New governments try to address these as well. Land reform is one of the most common requirements of justice in agricultural or pastoral societies. Human rights—whether of the first or the second generation[5] —especially for minority groups or a colonized majority, is equally high on the list. This level of justice usually takes longer to attain, since it requires parliamentary legal action. Economic aspects of structural justice are even more difficult to address, since no nation can any longer form economic policy in isolation from the rest of the world. Yet for long-term peace, addressing issues of structural justice is necessary for the long-term survival of peace.

A third level is legal justice, directed to the reform of law and of the judiciary. Unless law was completely suspended, both the legal code and the judicial system will have been compromised during the period of violence. Assuring a fair, open, and equitable legal system is an essential part of justice in the long term for the reconstruction of society.

---

[5]First generation human rights are political rights (freedom of speech and assembly, the right to elect one's leaders, etc.); second generation human rights are economic rights (right to food, clothing, shelter, work, etc.). On these, see Charles Villa-Vicencio, *A Theology of Reconstruction: Nation-Building and Human Rights* (Cambridge: Cambridge University Press, 1992), passim.

All this points to how complex justice is, and how difficult it may be to attain. That does not free us from the obligation to work for it, however. A new government that does not conspicuously struggle for justice will lose credibility in the eyes of its people. The temptation to be resisted is the quick administration of popular justice, that is, justice outside a legal system. Such crowd justice will perpetuate the evils of the past and could actually delay genuine justice being done.

Both truth and justice are essential to the reconciliation process. Because of the complexity of the past, it becomes important to be as clear as possible about what kind of truth and what kind of justice are being sought at any given time.

CHAPTER 11

Amnesty and Pardon

How does one finally come to terms with the past? In chapter 5, there was a discussion of forgiveness in its divine and human dimensions. Divine forgiveness is an extension of the love of God. Human forgiveness is a decision by a victim to no longer be controlled by the effects of past deeds done, and to choose freely for a different kind of future. One cannot forgive oneself, and one cannot forgive on behalf of the dead. Forgiveness does not eradicate the deed done; it is a declaration about one's relationship to the wrongdoer and to the effects of the deed. In other words, forgiveness does not erase the past or forget it. We do not forget the past when we forgive; we remember it in a different way.

Amnesty and pardon are the social and legal equivalents of forgiveness. Technically speaking, societies cannot forgive wrongdoers, since forgiveness is a moral act. Societies can grant amnesty or pardon, or they can decide to punish. But they cannot forgive.[1]

---

[1]Donald W. Schriver, Jr., in *An Ethic for Enemies: Forgiveness in Politics* (New York: Oxford University Press, 1995), talks about political forgiveness. The accounts he gives of putting the past behind a nation (or between nations) is very good, but one wonders how *nations* are able to do it. He defines forgiveness in the political context as "an act that joins moral truth, forbearance, empathy, and commitment to repair a fractured human condition." Shriver is speaking as an ethicist. I am not sure whether a nation can show empathy, for example.

Nor are amnesty and pardon the same thing. Amnesty, as the etymology of the word implies (from the Greek *amnestia*, "forgetfulness"), is a legal "forgetting" that the deed ever occurred. It means that whatever has been done will not be examined, nor will the alleged wrongdoer have to answer to any allegations or accept any blame or punishment for the deed. Amnesty has traditionally been used by victors to create a climate of good will in relations with the vanquished, effectively saying that their opposition to the victors has now been forgotten. This lays the groundwork for future cooperation. The Second Protocol of the Geneva Conventions (article 6.5) states that "at the end of hostilities, the authorities shall endeavour to grant the broadest possible amnesty."[2]

Pardon has a slightly different meaning. Legally, it means there will be no punishment. It does not imply "forgetting" that the deed occurred; it only says that the wrongdoer will not be punished. Technically, pardon leaves the door open for the possibility of hearings, or a trial and verdict. While this distinction is clear enough in law, in practice the distinction is often blurred, and the terms are used interchangeably.

Amnesty is used with great ambivalence in the face of human rights violations. On the one hand, some form of amnesty is often necessary to prevent a renewed eruption of violence. If a popularly elected government is restored after a military dictatorship, the military leaders may demand amnesty for themselves and their troops in return for not trying to overthrow the government again. Because of the continued strength of the armed forces, the civilian government may have little choice but to grant the amnesty. As has already been seen, at the cessation of hostilities in a civil war, both sides may need to be granted amnesty so that they can come together to rebuild the nation. Such was the case in El Salvador.

Amnesty may be used to elicit cooperation in finding out about the wrongdoing of the past. The Truth and Reconciliation Commission in South Africa could grant amnesty to indi-

---

[2]Cited in Daan Bronkhorst, *Truth and Reconciliation: Obstacles and Opportunities for Human Rights* (Amsterdam: Amnesty International, 1995), 100.

viduals who admitted and gave information about violations of human rights that they had committed. Amnesty here is used as a tool to get information to establish the truth about the past, information that could not be obtained in any other way. Here, amnesty works almost as a pardon, since the wrongdoer has to admit to what he or she has done.

Amnesties may make aspects of a reconciliation process possible (as with the Truth and Reconciliation Commission in South Africa), but in general they complicate the possibility of reaching reconciliation. Known perpetrators of human rights violations are allowed to continue their lives unscathed by the damage that they have wrought in society and in the lives of others. Amnesties for human rights violations weaken the new social order, and allow wrongdoers a continued power over society. Forgetting, in a moral sense, cannot be legislated or decreed. For victims or their families, amnesty often becomes an obstacle to individual reconciliation. Pardons may be hard to accept, but at least then there has been an admission of guilt.

Amnesties show that social reconciliation processes will always have to deal with compromise. A social reconciliation process almost never has the power to pursue its ends absolutely. Only courts of law aspire to that goal. For victims, compromise is experienced as acquiescence to the former power that victimized them. But sometimes, for the sake of a future order, such compromises have to be made, even though they make individual reconciliation difficult or seemingly impossible.

CHAPTER 12

The Church's Role
in the Reconciliation Process

The Church's role in reconciliation processes can be examined in two ways: in terms of the resources it brings to the reconciliation process, and in terms of the active role it can play in it.

What resources does the Church have to offer to the reconciliation process? I would suggest that there are three resources in particular that should be considered. The first is its message about reconciliation and the spirituality that flows out of it. The second is the power of its rituals. And the third is its capacity to create communities of reconciliation.

The Christian message of reconciliation and the spirituality that flows from it have been the subject of Part I of this book. The message was summarized in five points in chapter 1, with the subsequent chapters showing how the resurrection appearance stories of Jesus constitute instances where that message is embodied. It takes shape in a spirituality and a ministry of reconciliation that focuses on the plight of the victim and the restoration of the humanity of the victim. From this emerges a commission for the reconciled person to continue the reconciling work in the community and beyond.

The Christian message, and the spirituality that flows from it, also address issues such as memory, forgiveness, and the rebuilding of trust. Different perspectives can be taken on how to address these, but the Christian message has a coherence created by the stories of Jesus in which the message is embedded.

That makes it possible for victims to place their own stories in the story of Jesus, and with him become reconciled survivors. It is precisely the coherence of this message that can make it so useful to a divided society.

The Church has ritual that can be used in the process of reconciliation as well. Following 2 Corinthians 5:17, the Church believes that God has entrusted it with a ministry of reconciliation. The Roman Catholic Church expresses that ministry in the sacrament of reconciliation. The theology of this sacrament has yet to be fully brought to bear upon situations of social conflict, although progress is being made.[1] Pope John Paul II has explored the relation of justice, forgiveness, and reconciliation in a number of allocutions since 1995, but a connection with the sacrament has not yet been presented in any detail. Achievement of this will take collaborative work between theologians and those involved in social reconciliation. Mark Hay has suggested that one of the sacramental tasks in social reconciliation is dealing with the guilt of the bystanders. This is a promising suggestion that deserves to be put into practice.

The sacrament of reconciliation is not the Church's only ritual resource, however. It can make use of its space for important ritual moments that reach beyond the life of the Church to seal apologies, hear declarations of forgiveness, and celebrate movements into new places. It can in its preaching provide an ongoing schooling in the spirituality of reconciliation. And in its celebration of the Eucharist it can show the powerful symbol of the presence and the absence of the Lord, and how that heals memory and brings new hope.

Because of its moral standing in the community (providing that this has not been compromised utterly in the immediate past), the Church can create communities of reconciliation, those spaces of safety, memory, and hope that help make reconciliation possible. By accompanying victims, by creating zones of safety through hospitality, by unfolding memories, and by making new connections in the stories of victims, the Church can

---

[1] See Mark Hay, O.M.I., "Ukubuyisana: Reconciliation in South Africa" (D.Min. Thesis, Catholic Theological Union, 1997), chapter 3.

create a cadre of reconciled people who will serve as leaven in a new society. More important, by living as much as possible as a reconciled community, it can become a model to the larger society of what really is possible.

These three areas, then, are places where the Church offers resources that will help heal both individuals and society. Because each situation of reconciliation is different, the Church has to ask itself how and where its resources should be developed and shared.

Gregory Baum and Harold Wells's excellent collection, *The Reconciliation of Peoples: Challenge to the Churches*, details twelve case histories of the Church's involvement with reconciliation processes.[2] The book is a valuable compilation of experiences that offers many good hints as to how the Church can exercise in situations of social reconciliation the ministry of reconciliation which God has entrusted to it. The editors conclude that the Church rarely does this. Sometimes it is because of timidity, a fear that working to heal a divided society will introduce the divisions into the Church itself. Those divisions are likely already there, but are deftly kept from coming to the surface. At other times the Church fails to act out of guilt for its complicity in the violence—either through what it did or what it failed to do. The extent to which the Church succumbs to either fear or guilt is the extent to which it fails in its ministry of reconciliation. Churches should be trusting enough in the reconciling grace of God to admit their own failings and find ways of working toward reconciliation. Again, the Baum and Wells volume offers many suggestions.

How the Church might work on the national scale to effect reconciliation depends on the national circumstances. In places where the Church is a numerical minority, its presence may go largely unnoticed. Past histories of church-state relationships define also to some extent what roles might be available for agency in reconciliation.

The Church as an international organization has opportunities through its relief and development agencies, through its

---

[2]Gregory Baum and Harold Wells (eds.), *The Reconciliation of Peoples: Challenge to the Churches* (Maryknoll, NY: Orbis Books, 1997).

international religious orders, and through critical solidarity to work for reconciliation. Reconciliation could become one way of defining its mission in the world today.[3]

As elements of the reconciliation come to be understood better, it will be incumbent upon the Church to become more involved with its processes. The intensity of conflict that marks the end of the twentieth century is not likely to diminish in the first decades of the next. Reconciliation will be needed more, not less. With both spirituality and strategy, the Church must work with all people of good will to bring about the healing and transformation that shattered societies need.

---

[3]See Robert Schreiter, "Mission as a Model of Reconciliation," *Neue Zeitschrift für Missionswissenschaft* 52 (1996): 243-250.

INDICES

INDEX OF PERSONS AND SUBJECTS

INDEX OF SCRIPTURAL TEXTS